PRAISE FOR THIS BOOK

Are you seeking to live a more fulfilling life? If so, read this book and refer to it daily. Why? Because taking care of your psychic life is essential to your happiness —whether you consider yourself highly sensitive or not. *Everyone Is Psychic* offers a treasure trove of simple, practical, and effective tools, along with the author's wise experienced-based guidance. Ann O'Brien, intuitive teacher and Amazon #1 bestselling author, will help you awaken your intuition and know your inner self. She weaves in insightful stories from her personal experience to illustrate and give context to what she teaches throughout this user-friendly guide and workbook. Happy Reading—the book and others!

— **Michael J Tamura,** *Spiritual Teacher, Clairvoyant Visionary, Award-Winning Author of* <u>YOU ARE THE ANSWER</u>, *and Co-Host of Living The Miracle Internet Talk Radio*

Everyone Is Psychic is an engaging, encouraging and practical book based on the wisdom gleaned from Ann O'Brien's 17 years working as an intuitive, psychic and teacher. This book is both guidebook and a workbook, which allows what is read to be more fully integrated. The exercise and meditations are incredibly beautiful and can be returned to again and again. This is a book for anyone who wants to develop their inner connection to that wise part of themselves where truth resides, as well as those who have always had it but were not supported in being psychic in their families or felt odd for having it. This book not only normalizes psychic abilities but is all about cultivating and using them! This is incredible news because developing a strong psychic sense or deepening intuition is like having our very own GPS in life. The author's goal is to give insight into yourself by deepening this connection, and she does this like the wise Sage she is by offering tools to manage your psychic abilities.

Life is better in the flow, and listening to our psychic hits and learning to trust our intuition creates that flow. You will be grateful for having these gifts well honed. And you'll have *Everyone Is Psychic* to thank!

—**Catherine DeMonte,** *Psychotherapist, Energy Healer, and author of* <u>Beep! Beep! Get Out of My Way! Seven Tools for Powerful Creation and Living Your Unstoppable Life</u>

Ann O'Brien's work helps you grow your soul! This book will show you how to get grounded in this world, to discover your truth when you're afraid, to trust the Universe and to know that you have a purpose here on earth, and to allow yourself to bring in more joy, abundance and neutrality in life. *Everyone Is Psychic* is not just a psychic manual. It will help you live true-to-yourself in these wild times.

—**Wataru Hokoyama,** *Hollywood Film Composer and Energy Healer*

Everyone Is Psychic brilliantly brings clarity and understanding to what it means to be "psychic" so that we can all incorporate this aspect of being human into our daily lives and reap the benefits. By including thoughtful examples and explanations coupled with easy to follow yet powerful meditations, Ann O'Brien manages to distill her vast life experience as a professional psychic into a priceless guide for everyone. Whether you are just beginning to dip your toe into these waters or have been on this path for decades, this beautiful work will be a bounty of gems to discover and return to again and again.

—**Lynnette Suzanne Kenith,** *Tessitura Coaching & Energy Work*

As a brain-soul expert, I see how my clients hit roadblocks when there's energy stuck "in the field." This field is beyond the physical senses, which means that physical actions alone cannot always heal us. We are physical, mental, emotional and spiritual beings. I love how author Ann O'Brien describes psychic abilities in a way that everyone can understand. *Everyone Is Psychic* shows you how to hone your intuition and work with energy through simple, profound exercises and expert guidance. Waking up your intuition is a game-changer. I recall the day I realized that the healing of the soul and whole body required one *to listen to their intuition and trust it.*

I highly recommend this book if you are ready to create the love, success, health and happiness you desire and live as 100% YOU! What Ann O'Brien has released here is a practical guide that the world has been waiting for— and I believe we are finally ready for it. Filled with stories from her life, her teaching and nearly two decades working with clients, the author makes tapping into your intuition fun. Follow the exercises in *Everyone Is Psychic* and watch your life change!

— **Dr. Louise Swartswalter, ND, CBT,** *Brain-Soul Success Expert*

EVERYONE IS
PSYCHIC

*How to Awaken Your Intuition to Improve Your
Relationships, Enrich Your Life & Read Others*

ANN O'BRIEN

Publisher's Note

This book is intended to support you in your spiritual journey and self-healing path. That said, the meditation techniques, exercises and suggestions offered in this book are not promised or intended to take the place of medical, psychological or other professional services. Where expert assistance is needed, one should enlist the help of a qualified professional.

Copyright @ 2022 Ann O'Brien

Ann O'Brien Living
PO Box 1692
Carbondale, CO 81623

www.AnnOBrienLiving.com

All rights reserved. No part of this book may be reproduced or utilized in any form or by any means, electronic or mechanical, including photocopying, recording, or by any information storage or retrieval systems, without permission from the publisher. For information, write to living@annobrienliving.com.

Bible quotation is from the Modern English Version, accessed through www.biblegateway.com.

Book design by Lucinda Rae.

Name: Ann O'Brien, author.

Title: Everyone Is Psychic: How to Awaken Your Intuition to Improve Your Relationships, Enrich Your Life & Read Others

ISBN 978-1-7344128-2-6

*To all who are living the path of remembering,
choosing and sharing Light.*

CONTENTS

Acknowledgments ... xiii
Introduction ... xv

Chapter 1: Awakening to Who You Are ... 1
You're Not Crazy, You're Psychic ... 2
You Are a Spirit in a Body ... 5
How to Use This Book ... 7

Chapter 2: Demystifying Intuition ... 9
Everyone Is Psychic about Something ... 10
WRITING EXERCISE: Exploring Your Intuition ... 11
Common Blocks to Intuition ... 12
What Increases Your Psychic Abilities? ... 13

Chapter 3: Psychic Self-Care ... 17
Psychic Meditation 101 ... 18
Grounding Yourself ... 20
WRITING EXERCISE: What Makes You Grounded or Ungrounded? ... 21
MEDITATION: Using a Grounding Cord ... 22
The Importance of Replenishing Your Energy ... 24
WRITING EXERCISE: Discovering Where You Get Scattered ... 26
MEDITATION: Where Are You? ... 27
How to Call Your Power Back ... 28
MEDITATION: Reclaiming Your Energy ... 29
Clearing Your Head ... 30
MEDITATION: Claiming the Center of Your Head ... 31
Discovering Whether Your Feelings and Thoughts Are Yours ... 33
MEDITATION: Releasing What's Not Yours ... 36
WRITING EXERCISE: Why Are You Taking on Energy from Others? ... 38
MEDITATION: Letting Go of Your Unhelpful Subconscious Motivations ... 40
The Benefits of Feeling Your Feelings ... 41
MEDITATION: How to Work with Your Own Emotions ... 44
Energy Moves Faster Than Physical Reality ... 45

MEDITATION: Gauging a Specific Situation 47
Owning Your Truth 48
WRITING EXERCISE: Have You Been Honoring Your Truth? 50
Psychic Protection 51
MEDITATION: Setting the Energy in Your Home or Space 54
Spiritual Sovereignty 55

Chapter 4: Energetic Anatomy 57

What Is the Energetic Anatomy? 58
The Meanings of Different Colors 59
Chakras: Discovering the Energy Centers 61
MEDITATION: Clearing Your Chakras 65
The Aura and Aura Layers 66
PRACTICE: Sensing Another Person's Aura 68
MEDITATION: Setting Your Space Using Color 69
Cosmic and Earth Energy Channels 70
MEDITATION: Running Earth and Cosmic Energy 71
The Creative Rings 73
MEDITATION: Balancing Your Creative Rings 75

Chapter 5: Using Intuition for Yourself 77

The Power of Intention 78
How to Ask Good Questions 80
WRITING EXERCISE: Discovering Your Questions 82
Neutrality 85
MEDITATION: Finding Neutrality and Inner Freedom 87
Can You Learn to Predict the Future? 89
MEDITATION: Rose Readings for Specific Areas of Your Life 92
Are Your Decisions Your Own? 93
MEDITATION: How to Make a Decision Using Your Intuition 95
Understanding and Utilizing Your Dreams 96
MEDITATION: Healing Your Astral Body 98
Living in Flow 100

Chapter 6: Types of Intuition — 101

Quiz: What Are Your Natural Psychic Gifts? — 102
Clairsentience — 104
MEDITATION: Using Your Body as a Pendulum — 105
Telepathy — 106
MEDITATION: Clearing Your Telepathic Channels — 107
Clairaudience and Working with Spirit Guides — 108
MEDITATION: Meeting One of Your Guides — 111
WRITING EXERCISE: Getting a Message from Your Guide — 112
Clairvoyance — 114
MEDITATION: Empowering Your Clairvoyance — 115
Claircognizance — 116
MEDITATION: Awakening Your Inner Knowing — 117
Mediumship — 118
MEDITATION: Running White — 120

Chapter 7: Reading Another Person — 123

Be Playful — 124
Ethics and Integrity — 127
Reading with Purpose — 130
MEDITATION: Setting an Intention for Your Readings — 131
Choosing Your Reading Color — 133
PRACTICE: Giving a Rose Reading — 134
MEDITATION: Clearing and Replenishing after You Read Others — 135
Interpreting Energy and Communicating What You See — 137
The Art of Matching Energy without Merging — 138

Chapter 8: Special Reading Topics — 141

How to Practice These Readings — 142
Relationship Readings — 143
PRACTICE: Reading a Relationship — 144
Past Lives + Karma — 145
MEDITATION: Seeing a Past Life — 147

What Are the Akashic Records? ... 148
MEDITATION: Meeting Your Akashic Record Keeper and Updating Your Records ... 149
Connecting with Souls Who Have Passed ... 150
MEDITATION: Communicating with Spirits ... 152
Baby Beings ... 153
PRACTICE: Seeing Baby Beings ... 155
Psychic Kids ... 156
Energy Awareness Exercises for Kids ... 158

Chapter 9: Energy Healing and Manifesting ... 163

What Is Healing and When Do You Do It? ... 164
WRITING EXERCISE: When Have You Healed Unconsciously? ... 168
MEDITATION: Preparing to Heal ... 170
Addressing Health Issues ... 172
WRITING EXERCISE: Discovering the Energy Behind Your Health Issues ... 175
What Can You Heal Besides People? ... 176
PRACTICE: Healing a Specific Project, Space or Situation ... 177
Reading and Healing the Past or Future ... 178
PRACTICE: Reading and Healing Timelines ... 179
Why Do Painful Scenarios Repeat? ... 180
PRACTICE: How to Clear Karma with a Certain Person or Issue ... 181
The Power of Forgiveness ... 182
WRITING EXERCISE: Owning Your Part and Setting Yourself Free ... 184
How to Handle Interference ... 186
Understanding Unhelpful Mediumship and How to Work with It ... 188
MEDITATION: Healing Your Unhelpful Mediumship Agreements ... 192
Cycles of Creation ... 194
WRITING EXERCISE: Discovering How You Create Your Life ... 196
Keys to Manifesting ... 197
Conclusion ... 201
Resources ... 202
Your Intuition Journal ... 203

ACKNOWLEDGMENTS

Once you've read this book, you'll know one of my strong values is integrity. I have learned that integrity is not about only telling the truth and doing what you say. Integrity includes honoring what you are given.

Just before beginning this manuscript, my mother passed away. This—plus a couple other big events the same year—have pushed me to honor my life. I realized that my gifts to the world must be given.

"What am I good at? "I asked. "What have I been doing all my life? What do people say I help them with?" And I found myself staring at 10+ years of curriculums I have been teaching, which became this practical psychic manual.

And so first I would like to thank my mother, along with my father, my grandparents and all my ancestors. I thank you for the gift of this life as well as for the freedom to evolve.

As a mother to a highly engaged daughter, I revere in the silence whenever I get it. And so, I give thanks to Arthur, for showing up as her dad and supporting me to have this necessary space. On that note, I thank my daughter's teachers and everyone at her school as well as our community of friends. And I thank my daughter, who— even before she was conceived— told me, "Mama, I want you to keep doing your work."

To my psychic teachers and colleagues and friends—Michael and Raphaelle Tamura, Mary Bell Nyman, Hope Hewetson, John Fulton, Lynnette Suzanne Kenith and Lisa Waikalani, among others.

To those who directly helped me complete, publish and promote this book—Lucinda Raye for cover design, Robin Quinn for editing, and Mike Beas and team for marketing and formatting. For input along the way, my gratitude goes out to Kat Tepelyan, Megan Gaddis, Ayn Cates-Sullivan, Forrest Podrat and Susan Mitchell. Thank you to Zach Kasik at Wild Feather Recording and to Elysia Skye, for your fabulous work on the audio book.

To everyone at True Nature Healing Arts for your heartfelt support of me and my work, for hosting and promoting my sessions and workshops, and for creating such a beautiful energetic and physical space.

To all the healers and guides who have supported me in keeping my energy strong so I can give this gift.

To David Hooper, who gave me online marketing advice in exchange for psychic readings back in 2004, when I was on the brink of starting my business. I can still hear you saying, "Dude, you gotta have a blog." And so, I began writing about practical intuition. Thank you for giving me my first "gig," speaking to 50 musicians at the Nashville New Music Conference about how to manage the sensitivities that come with being an artist.

To Fred Beshid, for insisting I reserve www.EveryoneIsPsychic.com, 15 years before this book was ever conceived.

And most of all, thank you to all my clients and students over the years. Teaching and reading you has taught me almost everything I know about being psychic. I appreciate your sincerity in receiving this transmission, and I know that as you do, it will keep on giving.

INTRODUCTION

When I was a teenager, my mom took my friends and I to the new age shop. We would peruse the books and incense and it all felt a bit otherworldly. Was the lady at the counter a gypsy? I remember my mom buying me my first tarot deck when I was 15. She had no idea what it was, but I asked for it, so she got it for me. I spent countless hours laying the cards out on my bed, trying to understand my relationships. Instead of doing my homework, I learned to calculate astrology charts before the Internet could do it for you. I guess I didn't try that hard to seem "normal," because the boys at school teased one friend and I, calling us witches.

One day, my 11th grade physics teacher came in with a grocery bag full of astrology books (even though I didn't realize he had noticed any of this). He put the bag on my desk and said, "Have fun with these. I used to be into this stuff in college."

Somebody saw me! And then he went back to the chalkboard, and on with the class lesson.

This brief experience was one of the few I remember back then, where someone around me recognized the world of energy. Meanwhile, I felt some relief tapping into the mysticism in music, particularly psychedelic rock. I dove into writing and art and was always in love, seeking transcendence. I had a disdain for the superficial and for the ordinary, which I later learned to see as sacred too.

Flash forward to my 20s—when one of the things I learned in psychic school was how different my classmates and I were from average people. It was and it wasn't true. Everyone is psychic, yet at that time fewer folks were open to it. One teacher predicted a future where more people would wake up and seek healing. He said that our skillsets would be in high demand, and he was right. I feel so incredibly grateful that I got on this path early.

I remember pulling into my driveway one day, seven years after starting my business as an intuitive and healer, when it really hit me. "I am a professional psychic," I said to myself, a bit awestruck. Even though intuition was so much a part of me, using it as a job was not on my radar growing up. This was nothing the school guidance counselor would have recommended. And even in the first few years of my training, I really saw it as a hobby. Until it obviously was more than that.

This is a path that found me. No one really sent me on it. Quite the contrary, I stumbled around for a long time looking for mentorship. For years, those sporadic moments where the clouds parted and somebody spoke my language seemed like all I could hope for.

The world has changed. As I get ready to release this book, I share the title and subject with almost everyone I meet, and I haven't once felt crazy. We are ready for this in these unsettling times, in these times of so much light flooding in. We need our anchors, we need our inner compasses, and we are ready for creative options. Seeing more than meets the eye may now be just what gets us through today's uncertainty. Knowing how to live as all that we are, in our truth and in our bodies, is sure to bring grace no matter what life hands us.

It's an honor to now be the mentor to others that I needed so much back then. Thank you for sharing this journey with me.

Chapter 1:
AWAKENING TO WHO YOU ARE

YOU'RE NOT CRAZY, YOU'RE PSYCHIC

Spontaneous Psychic Experiences

I remember a sunny hotel pool and a heavy feeling. I was five, and my mom and sister and I were back in Florida after a year away. By the looks of it, this should have been a happy moment, but my dominant memory is that something was "off." Where was Dad? My parents were trying to protect us by not explaining their separation, but what I felt was not at all comfortable.

I remember being on a trip during college with some friends when an image popped in of my boyfriend hooking up with his ex-girlfriend. We never spoke of it and broke up after a few more months of feeling disconnected. Years later, he called and said, "There's something I need to tell you." And before he could, I told him exactly what had happened.

In my 30s, I put everything in storage and was traveling—looking for a new home. One morning in Durango, I woke up with the guidance to spend a month in Northern New Mexico. I had planned to drive to Santa Fe that day, and I knew I had a friend of a friend's couch to crash on for a few nights, but that was it.

On my drive down, I suddenly got the message to call my friend Lisa, who was visiting New Mexico around the same time. "Where are you?" she asked, and I told her. "Oh my gosh!" she said. "I'm on that same highway heading your way." We arranged to meet at a gas station, and I told her about my guidance to stay a month. She'd just left a Buddhist retreat house near Taos. "Interesting," she said, "the Lama who was scheduled to stay at the retreat until the end of the month just canceled. It's simple there, but if you want you could stay for a small donation." So, after my new friend's couch, I spent some time at the retreat, and it was the most blissful stop on my trip!

These are just a few stories of the "out of the blue" psychic experiences I have had, and as you can see, they weren't all as pleasant as that last example. As a kid, feeling what my parents felt was painful. And I didn't enjoy seeing what my college boyfriend was doing that night. I'm glad I wasn't in the dark, but ouch! Couldn't being psychic be a little easier?

I'm happy to say it's gotten much better over the years. This is not only because I've matured and become an adult, with much more choice in my experiences—though this helps. Setting intentions for my life has also harnessed my intuition, making it my friend instead of a demon to run from. Finding that place to stay in New Mexico was one of many powerful moments like this.

Moving from Fear and Overwhelm to Embracing Intuition

Intuition is not only for getting answers. It's also a pathway to freedom. It's saved me so much time and frustration because I've learned how to identify which thoughts and feelings are mine. I know how to release other people's stuff and work with my own. I've cleared a lot of old pain so that I can stay more grounded, and I don't need to go outside myself for answers as much as I used to earlier. Instead of being at the mercy of it 24/7, I now know how to turn my intuition on and off.

Here's how I like to explain it to the folks who look nervous in the front row when I teach: "Imagine going into Best Buy and watching all the TVs at once. You wouldn't want to, would you? And so, I'm not reading you all now; that would be overwhelming! I have a life." At this, people tend to laugh and relax.

Unfortunately, my childhood was like a trip through Best Buy. I had no filter; in fact, I didn't even know I was psychic. I had no real teacher until my mid-20s. Before that, I thought I was crazy when I asked my mom why she was angry, and she said she wasn't. I didn't know other people's emotions weren't my responsibility. And since I didn't know any other way to avoid feeling it all, I escaped into a dream world a lot.

I've been fortunate. Some who are psychic and don't know it turn to drugs or alcohol or other addictions. Some live with dark feelings or mean voices they don't know they can turn off. Others get sick or really do seem to go crazy. Many never find teachers or have the chance to explore this like I did. And so, I feel a calling to share.

Of course, get help if you need it, and meanwhile I hope this book can help you feel less crazy and more empowered. My goal is to give you both insight and practical tools to manage your abilities.

Ultimately, this stuff is fun! The more you see, the more you get free and the more you laugh. And then the more you get free and laugh, the more you see. You can use your seeing to better your life.

In this book, you'll learn to manage the energy you pick up without trying, as well as reconnect to more of your true self. I'll guide you through how to access your various psychic abilities to get practical answers about your life. Career, love, money, health and family matters are easier to handle when you have your own intuitive compass. We'll also delve into more esoteric subjects like past lives and spirit guides. Enjoy the journey!

YOU ARE A SPIRIT IN A BODY

Most of our preoccupations are "of the world." Your career, love life, family, money and health are all important. These are the arenas in which you learn, teach, experience joy and reap rewards. If you're like most people, one or more of these are fairly challenging, and one or more are relatively easy. It amuses me that for one person love is easy, yet money is hard, while another hardly thinks about money but struggles in love. Why? It rarely makes sense on the surface. Yet, it's a reminder that anything is possible, and we don't have to take our stuff so seriously.

We'll get into karma later in this book, and yet I'll touch on an important piece now: You are infinite. You are not your job, relationship or bank account. Nor are you your thoughts or emotions. Your body and everything you experience in the world are only vehicles to help you grow.

I believe we each chose the perfect body for what we are to experience. Our parents, birthplace and general life circumstances were mapped out ahead of time. You, the spirit, looked and chose the path that would best allow you to complete unfinished business, learn your lessons, and give your gifts. That doesn't mean you don't have free will; it just means you have had it longer than you can possibly remember.

Realizing your spiritual nature is key in finding inner peace. The more you are "in the world but not of it," the less attached you are to everyday conditions and the more your life will transform. Knowing yourself as an infinite soul is incredibly empowering. It means that whatever happens, you know you'll get through it.

As you remember all that you are, your psychic abilities also increase. You may already have had moments of feeling the interconnectedness of life. This expanded consciousness allows you to receive impressions beyond the 3-D. Having more of your spiritual freedom means you're less limited by desire or aversion.

Truly, developing your intuition is a spiritual path. It's fun and it's normal *and* it can take you really deep. Every reading I do helps me release my own triggers and blind spots, and then I see more clearly. In the Bible there is a saying: "First take the plank out of your own eye, and then you will see clearly to take the speck out of your brother's eye." (Matthew 7:5) When I see more in you, I see more in me and vice versa. Resisting nothing, there is so much joy.

HOW TO USE THIS BOOK

You've opened not only a guidebook, but a workbook as well. You may wish to do the exercises as you go. Or you may choose to read through the book, then go back and do the exercises. Some involve writing. Most are meditations, and so I recommend finding a quiet, uninterrupted space when you do them. Later in the book, I'll offer practices that allow you to read others.

The meditations can generally each be done in 10-15 minutes. Many people like to meditate early morning or last thing before bed, but don't stress—just find what works in your life. If it's in a parked car on your lunch break, do that! For a period of time, I meditated while nursing my daughter. As you gain experience with these exercises, you can do some of them on the fly when needed, with little effort or thought.

For best benefit, choose a meditation spot where you can sit upright with feet flat on the floor. This can be adjusted if your body or circumstances require.

While certain topics may pique your interest, I do recommend reading the chapters in order. I begin with some foundational concepts that will illuminate the later sections.

While you can easily go through this book on your own, you might like to read it at the same time as a friend, and then do the exercises together. This can help keep you accountable and validate your experiences. If you take this as a solo journey, you'll just need someone to practice your intuitive skills on in the later sections. That person may not be interested in reading or learning, and that's ok.

In the back of this book, I included an "Intuition Journal." You can begin using this now and add to it anytime you feel inspired. In this journal, you'll write down your intuitive impressions, what you did about them, and the result. This builds confidence.

Intuition gets stronger and feels more real the more we acknowledge it. It's easier to be open when the stakes are low. To explore, find things you're interested in, but not super-emotional about. For example, play with asking where you'll find a parking spot, when your favorite items are on sale, or what team will win a game. Note your answers and especially how many times you were right on target. Once you get some practice with lighter matters, you can explore deeper subjects with more confidence.

This is a process of discovering and fine-tuning a skill you already have. They say a fish can't tell you anything about water, and the average person can't tell you about being psychic. The reason is not because they're not. It's because we are all naturally psychic every second, in more ways than we know.

Let's talk about how to use your abilities, so they don't use you.

Chapter 2:
DEMYSTIFYING INTUITION

EVERYONE IS PSYCHIC ABOUT SOMETHING

I'd bet on it. You're already psychic about something. What do you spend your time thinking about? Even "ordinary" people who don't seem to be spiritual are psychic.

A mother feels what's going on with her children, even when they're in the next room. A skilled mechanic hears a tiny noise and knows what's going on with your car. Without measuring, a master chef adds the perfect seasoning, and somehow checks the pot just as it boils. And, a master coach gets a flash of a new direction for his client, with little prompting.

Technology is showing us what we already have inside. We've already been instantly interconnected; we just now have tools to validate this! And so, you might play with asking yourself who just texted you, before you look to see.

Imagine a conversation with someone and imagine their response back. Then, test your accuracy. At your next opportunity, ask that person what they think or feel about the subject you imagined speaking of. Record your findings in your Intuition Journal.

WRITING EXERCISE: EXPLORING YOUR INTUITION

Grab a pen and answer the following questions:

1. When in your life has your intuition helped you? What was going on at that time? What kind of space were you in?

2. When in your life have you ignored your intuition, then realized later it was right? Why did you ignore it? What was the result of doing so?

COMMON BLOCKS TO INTUITION

Though you're already psychic, being able to sit down and get answers to your personal questions at will may be challenging. We are often so intuitive that we have trouble distinguishing our impressions. However, entertaining the power of accessing your abilities whenever you want can bring up fears and doubts. Here are some of the most common blocks I see:

- Not wanting to be responsible, or feeling that you need to be, for what you receive
- Aversion to seeing something "negative"
- Afraid you'll be overwhelmed by the energy you pick up
- Subconscious or conscious memories of persecution (from this lifetime or others)
- Fear of your own power
- Self-doubt, "who me?" or feeling like you're making it up
- Not wanting to upset others
- Discomfort in being "different"
- Intuition just isn't in your comfort zone.
- Religious or intellectual programming

WHAT INCREASES YOUR PSYCHIC ABILITIES?

Many people think that being psychic is for rare, spiritually advanced people. While these abilities often appear as one deepens a spiritual practice, there are other reasons such abilities may be enhanced. As I see it, here are four top factors that impact intuition: (1) trauma, (2) genetics and biochemistry, (3) meditation and presence, and (4) acknowledgement.

Trauma

If people don't tell you what's going on, you need to find out somehow. Especially if your survival is at stake, being able to see what your eyes can't see or to hear what's not being said can be critically important. It's part of our human resilience that these innate abilities will come to the forefront when needed.

This can occur in subtle ways, such as my tapping into my parents' circumstances so that I could reconcile my feelings about what they weren't telling me. A more extreme example would be an abuse survivor who became psychic to keep himself safe, or to see his escape route.

If someone in your life has a problem with addiction, is naturally moody or becomes absent on some level—you'll likely develop methods beyond the physical to connect to them. This is also common when you're estranged from someone such as a family member or past lover.

In addition, the death of a loved one will cause many people to awaken their awareness of spirit. This could include seeing them in dreams, sensing their warmth, or imagining their comments when you think of them.

Spirits sometimes communicate through electronics and technology. Commonly, light bulbs will go out or flicker. Just after a death in a friend's family, his clock got stuck on the time the loved one died. A text she'd sent her husband almost a year prior suddenly came to the top of his messages. It said, "I'm having trouble getting home."

Genetics and Biochemistry

Heightened abilities run in the family. While they didn't pursue it professionally, my dad and my sister have similar abilities as me. For example, I used to play "the psychic game" with my dad. I'd give him a name— without any other information— and see what he felt intuitively about the person. Once, I named of one of my singer/songwriter friends and my dad said, "He thinks he's Barry Manilow." I giggled because not only was this guy a singer, he also physically resembled Barry Manilow and had a somewhat similar musical style. My dad had never met him!

If you have intuitive experiences, think about and/or ask who else in your family has them too. Or know that if other family members have them, it will likely be easier for your skills to develop.

Diet and lifestyle also play a role. It's not so simple as me telling you what to eat, because each person's needs and circumstances are unique. Some may need more grounding foods and others do best with juicing and eating lighter to unclog their channels. That said, sugar and alcohol tend to be extremely expansive, and when this happens, you have less choice over what energies come in. It's not that you wouldn't be psychic; you just might not like what you're picking up. I recommend using these substances in moderation and with discernment, if you are going to use them.

Whichever foods you choose, I do recommend eating clean and organic whenever possible. Chemicals, GMOs and highly processed foods can decrease your sensitivity because your body has to work harder to handle these unnatural substances. Personally, I'm fond of eating a small square of dark chocolate before each reading! They say chocolate supports the pineal gland, which aids the third eye.

Your environment can support or detract from your intuitive capacities, as well as influence what you receive. How do you feel when you watch the news or spend time on social media? Are you constantly around WIFI, Electromagnetic Fields (EMFs) or pollution? What is the prevailing mindset in your social group, family or workplace? All of this influences you, and while it is not necessarily physical, it is vibrational.

And there is a profound correlation between the vibrations you take in and your biochemistry. If the vibrations are negative or staticky, it will be difficult for you to receive higher guidance.

Meditation and Presence

Taking time each day to be still has profound impacts. You could do a formal meditation practice, take a walk, or turn off your phone when you need to unplug. Perhaps try different things and see what works. In this book, I'll be giving you lots of meditations that specifically enhance your intuition. I trust in their effectiveness, and I use many of them when I work with clients. I also get a lot of my personal answers anytime I have quiet time alone. If I'm feeling stuck trying to figure something out or just lacking inspiration, it often comes when I'm washing dishes, driving, exercising or resting.

When you're first starting or if you wish for more personal balance along with your psychic gifts, I definitely recommend practicing the meditations offered here. Beyond that, the really important thing is creating space in your days, weeks and life. You must find space in relationship to your emotions and other people, in the midst of tasks and conversations and information—if you are to see anything clearly. We'll get into that in this book—just how to find this space. And in principle, this means you must discover yourself as a spiritual being who *has* a human life. If you think you *are* all your emotions and thoughts or if you get lost in activity or other people's energy, it's next to impossible to find peace or clarity.

Acknowledgment

You might make an incredible dinner or do an amazing job on a project. If no one notices, you may be happy, but not that inspired to do it again or figure out how you did it. However, if everyone at the party raves about your dinner, you'll be digging up recipes and thinking about what you're going to make the next time. When your project gets praised at a big work meeting, you'll surely want to keep giving your best, so you meet or exceed people's expectations. Acknowledgement creates motivation, and motivation means you'll persevere, so your skills increase.

When it comes to your intuition, seeing is believing. If you imagine a friend needs help and then call and find it's true, you're more likely to notice these types of impressions next time you have them. When your body says, "Turn left" and you find out you avoided an accident, or if an idea flashes in your mind that turns out to be extremely lucrative—you'll start trusting your intuition more.

I highly recommend using the Intuition Journal in the back of this book to keep track of your progress. If you have a friend who is also doing this practice, you can compare notes and help support one another. Having someone to share your breakthroughs with makes this much more fun! If you don't have this in your life or would like to meet more like-minded souls, check out my website (mentioned in *Resources* in the back of the book) for upcoming classes and programs.

Chapter 3:
PSYCHIC SELF-CARE

PSYCHIC MEDITATION 101

I started meditating at 18, when my college offered a month-long immersion in Far Eastern religions. I loved the peace and self-reflection of Zen practice. Right after college, I lived in a tent for seven weeks and immersed myself in a yogic lifestyle. Besides the Ayurvedic diet, ethical principles and philosophies, I explored new types of meditation, breathing and purification practices. I moved to Boulder and continued the practices on my own for about six months before I got sick and quit meditating. While my intuition came online and I felt frequent bliss during my morning practice, I couldn't cope with my job at a preschool handling two-year-olds' tantrums. There was one particular meditation where we were taught to expand our energy field to the size of the Universe. No one had taught me how to come back to my body. I'm sure that meditation is lovely for some people some of the time, but at that moment it was not for me! I got completely overwhelmed.

There are a lot of great ways to meditate. Prior to my psychic training, the methods I learned didn't involve the body much. By contrast, the psychic meditations I teach are almost all "in-body" practices. This is why we sit with our feet on the floor, to connect with the earth and to give ourselves a place to "land." We do a lot of guided visualization and energy exercises. While the practices are easy-to-follow, they are dynamic and engaging. For me personally, they have allowed me to work with my energy in a way that simply sitting and watching my breath never did.

If you are not naturally visual, or if you don't see things exactly as I describe them, don't worry. Intention is enough. If you feel rather than see, or if you see a beam of light when I tell you to picture a waterfall, it's ok. Your soul may have its own language, and some skills just take practice. Trust what works for you and don't get stuck in the details.

When we come into the body and move energy, the following are common experiences: yawning, eyes watering, getting sleepy or feeling warm or cool. These are signs of healing. Stay present and celebrate them the best you can.

If you are feeling tired or angry or sad and you've been repressing it, these meditations will bring it up for you to experience. This is ultimately helpful, though not always comfortable.

As you clear past memories from times that you "spaced out," you may feel spacey. Students sometimes feel bad that they fell asleep or couldn't remember a thing that I said during a meditation. Typically, this happens when old unconsciousness is leaving your space, and it means little about what's actually happening now. If you experience something like this, my advice is to breathe and let it move. Know that your soul still received the meditation. You can always do it again if you wish to bring more conscious awareness to it.

Go slow if you need to and be gentle with yourself.

GROUNDING YOURSELF

Before you begin consciously awakening your intuition, I recommend learning to ground. A grounding cord is like a drainpipe, an energetic connection between you and the center of the earth. Having a grounding cord allows you to release everyday stress, other people's opinions or emotions from your past. It helps you find your foundation, which brings ease as you go through life. If you were a tree with a root system miles-deep, would you care if a gust of wind came?

Many naturally intuitive people spin out, get overwhelmed, or have challenges in work or relationships if they do not learn how to ground themselves. Here are the top reasons I suggest grounding:

1. So that it's safe to open and receive
2. To release energy that's not yours
3. So that you feel more secure and able to handle things
4. To reduce overwhelm, depression and anxiety
5. To bring your intuition visions and desires into physical reality

Sleeping and eating well, exercise and time in nature are great ways to ground. Anything that brings you into your body, in the present moment, can be grounding.

Each of us has personal habits that either support or detract from our grounding. When you're easily triggered, anxious or feel "all over the place," those are indicators that you've lost your balance. By contrast, feeling peaceful and able to handle whatever comes your way are signs of being grounded. In the next exercise, please explore your personal habits that either support or sabotage you in this area.

WRITING EXERCISE: WHAT MAKES YOU GROUNDED OR UNGROUNDED?

1. What helps you feel present and at peace? Write down everything you can think of such as diet and nutrition, self-care practices, activities you love, etc.

2. What tends to throw you off-balance? This could include social or environmental influences, habits that compromise your well-being, and diet or lifestyle choices.

MEDITATION: USING A GROUNDING CORD

- Find a cozy place to sit with your feet flat on the floor and your spine upright.
- Exhale, soften your body, and gently allow your breath to flow all the way out. At the end of the outbreath, notice your belly drawing in towards your spine.
- Inhale, sit taller, and observe your belly, diaphragm and heart getting fuller.
- Continue this breathing pattern at a relaxed pace, without effort.
- Snuggle your sit bones into your chair or cushion and feel your feet.
- Imagine a tree trunk, waterfall, or beam of light connecting your tailbone to the center of the earth. Make it as wide as your hips, fully connected and rooted. Breathe, let go, and feel the security of this "anchor" to Mother Earth.
- Let your breath flow out and imagine a trap door opening at your pelvic floor. Allow gravity to draw out of you anything that is not yours to hold. That could be the stress of your day or week, your loved ones' emotions, or energy you picked up from the world. If it's not yours, it has to go as soon as you simply decide to release it.
- You can also release old stories, past trauma and unhelpful beliefs or pictures. Sometimes you won't know what you're letting go of, but you'll feel better after the fact.

Be forewarned that grounding can make you tired. If you need more rest, getting into your body like this will certainly bring your fatigue to your attention! That's not a bad thing. Whatever your body needs, grounding will let you know.

I recommend checking your grounding cord once a day, or anytime you feel "off." Check to be sure it's going all the way down to the center of the earth, and that it's fully sealed both there and at your hips. You might widen it or imagine clearing other people and energy out of it. On occasion, it may be appropriate to completely release your grounding cord and make a brand-new one. That waterfall from yesterday may not provide the stability you need today, or the tree trunk you used to love might be too rigid when emotions get stuck. Your grounding cord can be anything that conducts energy. Have fun, stay tuned, and get creative!

It's also really fun and useful to ground other things besides yourself. Try it on your phone, your car, your credit card, your food, your computer or your to-do list. Notice how these things work better, feel better, or become more effortless.

THE IMPORTANCE OF REPLENISHING YOUR ENERGY

The first time I worked with Jennifer, she confessed that she was scared her boyfriend was cheating on her. I didn't think he was, but I saw the problem. Her energy was not in her body, but instead it was off with her boyfriend, tracking his every move. Jennifer felt very unsettled because she had abandoned herself in attempt to keep checking on him. Not only that, but her partner was not attracted to a woman who was lifeless and anxious. He wanted her to be sensual, open and in her body. Because of all this, Jennifer's fears could have become a self-fulfilling prophecy if she didn't shift something.

We spent just 30 minutes on Zoom, and the main thing we did was call her energy out of her boyfriend's space and back to herself. The next day, she emailed me in awe: "He came home and said, 'What did you do tonight? You look SO beautiful.'" Jennifer and I did many more sessions over the years, but that was the last time we talked about her feeling jealous.

After grounding or releasing energy, I always recommend replenishing. There is a Universal law that says every empty space will be filled. If you let go of something and do not choose what to replace it with, it will be replaced with whatever's around. The energy you just got rid of is likely to come back if you don't decide otherwise. The static in the world is ever-present and will seep in if you aren't conscious, yet it doesn't have to affect you.

Let's imagine your body is a house. If you left the doors and windows open and weren't home for months, would you be surprised to return and find it full of homeless people and pizza boxes? If you go out for the afternoon and come back—no problem! We all space out from time to time. Yet if you're habitually "out," whoever moves into your house starts to take over and it becomes harder and harder to get your space back. Many of us have given up our seniority to Mom, Dad, partner, boss or other influences in our environment without realizing it. The good news is that your body is still yours, and there are ways to discover and clear this energy and come back to yourself.

Commonly, we check out in moments of pain. While initially this feels like an escape, it generally backfires because our lack of presence invites more energy to enter our field. The last thing we need in a difficult scenario is more of whatever's hurting us! Paradoxically, breathing and being with the pain causes it to diminish *in most cases*. Of course, if you need to get away for physical or other reasons, just come back to your body and breath as soon as you're able. Perhaps do some extra energy clearing or get some support.

In the next exercises, I'll guide you to explore why you may leave your body and all the subtle ways this can happen. For example, it's common to get scattered during travel, while dreaming of other places, or even in everyday transitions, such as going from home to work or doing errands. Also, you leak energy when you over-focus on where things are going or when you're not at peace with the past. In addition, you may be giving your power to others by wondering what they think of you, wanting something from them, or allowing them to emotionally trigger you.

We all get at least a little bit scattered every day, so it merits regular attention. It does not need to be a big deal unless we neglect our need to replenish after something big occurs—or after a lot of little energy leaks add up.

WRITING EXERCISE: DISCOVERING WHERE YOU GET SCATTERED

List all the places you can think of where you may have left your energy. Have you left it with other people, in places distant or near, in the past (such as in memories, regrets or trauma), in the future (perhaps in hopes, dreams, fears or expectations)? Write down whatever comes to mind.

MEDITATION: WHERE ARE YOU?

You know where your body is. But where are you, the spirit? If you, like most of us, aren't always fully present, you may not notice this. Here's a meditation to help you start to recognize where your attention goes:

- Sit quietly, breathe and create a grounding cord.
- Imagine bringing your attention to a point in the middle of your head just behind your physical eyes.
- Create this space in your head as a sacred space just for you. You could imagine you're in a bubble of light, in a sanctuary-like room, or a spot in nature. Whatever you choose, see it as a lovely, clear space where you are at peace.
- Then, as your body sits in the chair, imagine going up to the corner of your actual room. Take your awareness there and look down at your body. What do you experience here?
- Then, pop back into the center of your head. Be aware from there and observe what it's like being in that space.
- Repeat several times so that you get a feeling for the difference between the two spaces. Is one of these spaces more familiar?
- When you feel complete, come back to the middle of your head, take a moment to connect to your body and your grounding, then open your eyes.

HOW TO CALL YOUR POWER BACK

The gold sun meditation that I'm about to share is a tool to call all of your power, creativity, attention and energy back to you. When you do this, please note that you are not bringing back your past problems, nor are you filling up with the judgements you sent to others. Instead, the energy you reclaim comes back neutralized as pure life-force energy. You are calling your power back, not the specific emotions or situations.

I end every private session with this meditation, and my clients are often surprised at how powerful it is. They'll spend an hour asking me for answers and clearing, which is super helpful. Yet, once they feel their energy coming back from everywhere it's been, they often say that this was the best part of their session.

Your gold sun can also be used to manifest the things you'd like for yourself. It is a way to draw in all that is meant to be yours, in grace… in the most perfect ways. The Universe is infinite, and I recommend making room for happy surprises.

MEDITATION: RECLAIMING YOUR ENERGY

- Sit, close your eyes, and ground yourself.
- Imagine a big golden sun a few feet above your head, about three times as big as your physical body.
- Inside the sun, picture a magnet that attracts all of your energy back from people and places, the future or the past. Decide that this energy comes back neutralized as pure life-force energy.
- See this energy returning from all around as rays of gold light, and as it does, notice the sun getting bigger, brighter and more radiant.
- Allow this sun to call to you all that is meant to be yours by Divine right, including happy surprises.
- Consider anything you'd like for yourself, including not only material things but also how you want to feel. Without putting anyone's name or face on it, visualize these experiences coming your way and put those desires in your gold sun.
- With everything you're calling in, I recommend adding "This or something better, in grace in the most perfect way."
- When you're ready, let the golden light pour down through your crown like liquid. Allow it to flood every cell of your body as well as your energy body with light, replenishing any places where you need it. Let it go down to your tailbone, toes and fingers. See it expand beyond the edges of your skin until it creates a golden bubble around your body—front and back, left and right.
- Open your eyes and notice your radiant self!

CLEARING YOUR HEAD

If you tend to be emotionally overwhelmed, confused or lacking in certainty, I recommend regularly clearing out the center of your head so you can claim that space. Our heads can seem like a jumble of thoughts, voices and problems to analyze. That's why it's such a powerful place to go. I am asked a lot, "Shouldn't I be in my heart, or in my body?" Yes, and…

You may have heard or believed that you should "get out of your head" in order to be spiritual. Yet when I talk about your head, I don't mean your analytical mind. Your brain, as I see it, is part of your body. You are not all those fluctuating thoughts. You are an infinite spiritual being, and you can rest in that space behind your eyes anytime you like. You can watch the world from there.

When I lead clients in the following exercise, they report feeling less stuck, freer, and more relaxed around things that were bothering them. Triggers disappear, and life feels more spacious and less pressured. Suddenly, they see clearly where things had been muddy. Even better, they feel empowered. Let's try it.

MEDITATION: CLAIMING THE CENTER OF YOUR HEAD

- Sit in a comfortable place for meditation, with your feet flat on the floor.
- As you inhale, let your spine lengthen as you sit taller. As you exhale, soften your body and feel your sit bones snuggling into your chair or cushion.
- Say hello to your grounding cord, and then allow yourself to release any energy you don't need down to the center of the earth.
- Remember the infinite being that you are.
- As that being, find that sanctuary space in the middle of your head that you found before. You might start by visualizing a point of light between your ears and behind your eyes. Bring your conscious awareness to that point, and then decide that you can observe everything from there.
- Let this space become larger until you see a beautiful room, a bubble of light, or a natural setting around where you sit.
- Notice: is there anyone in this space with you? If so, they often just want to be seen. Say hello and see if they go. If not, ask them politely and remind them that this is your head. Encourage them to find their own answers and whatever they need in their own body and life. Or, let them know you'll talk with them later, after your meditation time. In most cases, one of these approaches will work.
- When you have visitors in your head that don't leave when you ask, you may have an unconscious agreement or resistance that lets them in. An agreement could be something like "I agree to share everything with my sister," and so you always let her in. As for resistance, if you have a belief like "Men are slimeballs and I want nothing to do with them," boom—your charge around men will attract the very energy you're hoping to push away.
- Ask if you have any agreements or resistances that are keeping unwelcome visitors in your head. If so, send some gold light through your head to clear it out. Then, see your guests go back to their own

spaces.
- Keep affirming that this is your head, keep seeing your personal sanctuary, and keep setting it at your vibration. Ultimately, this will preserve this space for yourself.
- While you're in this pure space of witness, consider a problem you've been having. This could be a relationship or work issue, a condition in your body or mind, or something else. Decide that you can *watch* that problem from inside your head. Notice that however it has seemed, you are *not* that problem. You are aware of it perhaps, but you are still you—a pure, clear spark of consciousness that is always at peace. Enjoy this for as long as you would like.
- When you're ready, visualize a huge golden sun above your head, three times as big as your physical body. Draw all your light and love into it from everyone and everywhere you've been, from all points in time. Let that sun saturate your body and energy body until you feel full. Then, come out of meditation.

DISCOVERING WHETHER YOUR FEELINGS AND THOUGHTS ARE YOURS

During the year-long clairvoyant program I took in the late '90s, my friends thought I was learning to be psychic. Ha! I thought so too, until a few months in when I realized I'd been psychic all my life. That wasn't what I needed to learn.

Month after month, I was unpeeling layers of thoughts, emotions and programs I'd believed were mine. Yet I realized I didn't need to *process* as much as I thought I did. Being as sensitive as I was, that was a huge relief! I also became more efficient in what I did process, because here's the rule of thumb: *If you can't process it, it's not yours.*

For example, when you cry and feel better, that was your sadness. If expressing anger gives you clarity, or if fear subsides after you notice it and take appropriate measures—those were your feelings.

Getting stuck in an emotional black hole—like you can't stop bawling or raging or shaking with anxiety no matter how much you try to work through it—that's indicative that you've taken on other people's stuff. If you wake up bright and shiny, then become fussy after you talk to that friend or go do those errands—those are clues you're picking up foreign energy. When your emotions make no sense, I suggest asking where they came from before trying to "solve" them.

I remember when my former mother-in-law and I disagreed about whether my then-toddler could watch TV. She thought I should recognize the special relationship a grandparent has with her grandchild and let her do as she wished. I felt she should respect my boundaries as a mother. After a short conversation and email exchange, I had trouble sleeping for three nights as the issue kept circling through my mind.

Finally, I spoke with one of my intuitive friends who suggested I clear my mother-in-law's energy out of my head. In the midst of my own life, I had forgotten to do what I teach others! Once I did that, I slept soundly and practically forgot about the matter.

A participant in one of my workshops spoke to the power of

releasing what's not yours when she emailed me to say, "Ann, thank you so much for the meditation on clearing stuck emotions! I only listened to that one class so far, and right after I did, my teenage stepdaughter texted me in hysterics.

"Her mother has borderline personality, and she was trying to guilt her for having a birthday party. My stepdaughter couldn't shake the energy, so I called her and listened to her cry uncontrollably. After a few minutes, I offered to lead her in that meditation. I said, 'I've only just learned this, but are you open?'

"She said, 'Yes, I'll try anything!' and so I suggested she imagine the gauge you taught us, to find out what percentage of the energy she felt was hers. She took her time to look and then said the gauge showed it was only 1% her emotions. We then did the clearing exercise and she felt SO much better."

When you have a conversation or thought pattern spinning nonstop in your head, like a record stuck in a groove, it's not yours. By contrast, your own problems feel like creative challenges. They're not always simple or fun, but you get somewhere when you think about them. Additionally, you're able to turn these thoughts "off" when you need to focus on something else.

The good news is this: It's much easier to release other people's energy than it is to process it. When an energy is not yours, as soon as you let it go, it's gone. It's like having a puzzle piece to someone else's puzzle and you'll want to release it because:

1. It makes you feel crazy.
2. The other person can't heal this piece as long as you're holding it for them.
3. You holding it generally pushes the other person away, because they see the parts of themselves that they rejected in you.

When emotions belong to you, I do recommend feeling them, so they don't get stuck in your body. When something is yours, you have to feel it and process it through the body. It's more about transforming it than it is about getting rid of it. Some ways to do this are to talk or write about it, scream in your pillow, get bodywork, move or dance. I'll share a meditation later that will give you a place to start.

To any issue, there are usually multiple layers that often take time to come to the surface. You will see progress when you feel lighter and clearer and notice how the "charge" you've had around your issue gets released. Remember that sometimes healing is like peeling an onion—as you take away one layer, a new one gets revealed. Be loving and patient with yourself, and practice!!

The following meditation will assist you with letting go of the energy that's not yours.

MEDITATION: RELEASING WHAT'S NOT YOURS

When you discover you've been processing energy that belongs to someone else, this exercise will help you let it go. In addition, you can use this meditation to release anything from your past that is no longer helpful to hold. If you're not sure what's wrong but you feel off or stuck, this is also an excellent practice!

- Sit upright with your feet flat on the floor.
- Check in with your breathing and grounding cord, making sure it's connected to both your hips and the center of the earth.
- Consider the situation you feel stuck on, or the thoughts or emotions that won't seem to go away.
- Imagine a bubble a few feet in front of you, like a magic soap bubble with a magnet in it.
- Decide that the bubble will pull out any energy that's not yours with respect to this problem or pattern.
- Include any past triggers, stories, memories, beliefs or emotions that aren't serving you. Let these go as well.
- Exhale and notice any pictures, messages or sensations you experience as this is happening. You may be aware of a shift in a certain part of your body, or perhaps you see someone's face or a scene in your mind's eye.
- If you're called, move the bubble up or down or around your body, anywhere it needs to go to clear what you need to clear.
- Once you feel complete, stay in your body as you watch the bubble float off to the edge of the horizon. See it pop and dissolve.
- Now, let go. Don't wonder anymore about what you discarded; otherwise, it's like you're chasing the trash truck down the street. Be in your body and be happy it's gone.
- Doing this exercise sends energy back where it belongs. If you released someone else's feelings, they just got a healing by getting their energy back. This ultimately empowers them as well as you.

- Complete this meditation by filling in with a golden sun and revitalize the places you just emptied. Call your power back from wherever it's been.

WRITING EXERCISE: WHY ARE YOU TAKING ON ENERGY FROM OTHERS?

Energy does not just invade your space without your permission. I realize it's hard to accept this when you feel like a victim. However, taking responsibility for your part is necessary in changing the pattern.

Consider where you get the most triggered. Is it around someone you know, a specific type of person, or in a certain environment?

In each case, ask why you let this get to you. When you allow something outside yourself to affect you, there is always something you're getting out of it. For example: Are you healing others so that you get validation, or so they take care of you in some way? Have you taken on your dad's lack of ambition so you don't outshine him, or your friends' beliefs so you can feel like you fit in? Does whatever you're taking on reinforce a subconscious expectation or story you've been repeating?

Sometimes we're motivated by true needs, and yet we end up choosing toxic patterns to get them met because we don't know a better way. For example, if you believe you're not good enough, you may attract people who put you down. You might also become someone you're not in pursuit of success, and then end up feeling even worse about yourself. Perhaps you want someone to love you, so you put your attention on them and end up feeling however they're feeling—even if this actually hurts you. Or you crave sweetness, and so eat too much sugar instead of taking a bath and buying yourself roses.

Once you discover what motivated you, it's easier to forgive yourself. Then you can explore how to get that need met in a healthier way. The following writing exercise will help you find power and freedom through this process:

1. Note a few times when you absorbed other people's thoughts or emotions. You might also write about a pattern you have—for instance, you do it with a specific person, in a particular environment, or at a certain time.

2. Write down what you thought you would get by taking this energy on. Consider unhealthy motivations as well as true needs.

3. Can you think of any healthier ways to meet these needs? Record them here.

MEDITATION: LETTING GO OF YOUR UNHELPFUL SUBCONSCIOUS MOTIVATIONS

Here, you'll repeat the "bubble" mediation, this time to get free of the unhelpful motivations you just wrote down.

- Sit, close your eyes, and see your waterfall or tree trunk connecting your hips to the center of the earth.
- Breathe and consider what's been driving you to pull in energy that's not yours. Remember what you wrote down earlier and be open to new awareness and additional clearing.
- Imagine a magnetic, magic soap bubble a few feet out in front of you.
- Let this bubble attract all the subconscious motivations, stories and beliefs that have caused you to pull in unhelpful energy from others. Let the bubble absorb all you are ready to release, taking the bubble all around your body if this seems helpful.
- What impressions are you getting about what's clearing? You may receive pictures, feelings, words or just an inner knowing.
- Once you feel complete for now, let the bubble float off into the distance until you see it go "poof" in a burst of light.
- Create a giant gold sun above your head. Place a magnet in the sun, and let this magnet attract your creative life force back from other people and places, future and past. Before you bring it in, also put the feeling of having your true needs met into the gold sun. Be open to any messages of how that can be accomplished.
- When you feel ready, draw this golden light through the crown of your head into every part of you, and then open your eyes.

THE BENEFITS OF FEELING YOUR FEELINGS

While it does no good to try resolving other people's stuff in your body, your own emotions absolutely need your attention. Of course, do your best to feel them in a way that's appropriate. I recommend dedicating a space and time and be sure you're not harming anyone or anything in the process. You may have occasional days where you need to cancel plans so you can process something. Otherwise, consider what you can do for maintenance—such as regular workouts or journaling sessions, so things don't get pent up.

It may be tempting to brush things under the rug or to power through your feelings, but unfortunately this is more likely to make them fester and grow. This can cause health problems as well as relationship challenges or blocks to manifesting. The thing you are avoiding tends to control everything around you. By contrast, feeling what you feel tends to free up energy and power like you wouldn't imagine.

I remember lying in bed crying many years ago, about something that had been bottled up. Right then the phone rang, and I was surprised I hadn't turned the ringer off. I had a split second to wonder, and then my instincts said, "Answer." Thankfully I did, because it was a well-regarded yoga studio offering me a job. It was an opportunity I'd been working towards for years, and I believe that moving my tears made room for it to come in.

A few months before I got pregnant, I had a big talk with my mom. My anger at her had been building for years, particularly since hearing my dad's side of the story about my childhood. I resented her not being there for me in certain ways, and I called her out for blaming him. I hadn't enjoyed her programming, guilt-tripping and not speaking up about her needs. I let her know I would not be repeating these patterns, and that I felt called to share for the purpose of healing. For sure, it was an awkward conversation. Yet once we got through it, all that "stuff" that used to weigh down our relationship was just not there. Things became easy between us.

I didn't know at the time how quickly I'd be pregnant. Once I was, I was able to receive support from both my mom and other women in a new way. Previously, unlike many people who craved "mother energy," I hadn't really believed that the feminine could nurture me. This was my blind spot until late-stage pregnancy. At that time, a highly intuitive woman cooked for me, and I remember how revolutionary it was to receive these lovingly prepared meals each week. When I gave birth, due to serendipity we had four women there by my side. I never would have chosen this, but it was a profound awakening that allowed me to receive more and appreciate my own feminine as well. The day my daughter came into the world, the house seemed flooded with light, and her birth was smooth and healthy. I felt elated. I'm sure I released some toxic emotions by speaking up with my mom, which helped clear the way for such a beautiful experience.

Last year, my mom passed away. As soon as I heard she was sick, I knew she was on her way, and that we were at peace. As our relationship came full circle, I felt immensely grateful that I had done my part so she could go this way.

It's common to want to make our feelings wrong when we feel vulnerable. This is true not only for the obviously painful emotions—like grief or anger—but even for joy or desire, which our life or culture may not seem to have a place for. It's like many of us learned to live with the thermostat set at a certain temperature or the radio playing one style of music, when in fact there are many options.

Every emotion has its messages. Anger indicates that either you or someone else has violated your boundaries. This offers clarity. Grief leads to a deepening, compassion and freedom. Jealousy shows you what you want to have or be. And joy, I believe, is a natural expression of your true self. All of these are incredible gifts that I wouldn't want to be without.

Living as a fully-feeling being offers freedom and lightness. What does this have to do with being psychic? Being psychic means seeing what's true, seeing the unseen. There's no way you can avoid noticing emotions once you awaken your abilities. As an infinite spiritual being, you already include it all. Emotions want to move and create something. So I suggest letting your feelings flow so you can harness their energy before they create a dam. They are a sacred part of you.

MEDITATION: HOW TO WORK WITH YOUR OWN EMOTIONS

This exercise is to move emotions that *are* yours. Many people aren't sure how to do this, so here's one exercise:

- Lie down, sit or stand in a relaxed position.
- Soften and feel yourself drop into your body on each exhale.
- Now, become aware of any emotions that arise, or reflect on those you've had lately. This may come easily, but if not, scan your body for any areas that feel tense or "off." Sometimes you'll notice an overall state such as sluggish, agitated, tingly, cold or energized.
- If you have a health issue or pain in a certain place, check in there.
- Ask this body part—or condition within your body—if it has a message for you. If it could speak, what would it like to say? Be aware not only of "hearing" a message but also of physical sensations, imagery, or a sense of feeling or knowing. Let it express fully.
- Ask what color will heal this part of your body or this state within your body. Breathe into it while imagining sending color there.
- Next, where in your body do you feel open? Is there a particular spot or an overall sense of pleasure anywhere? Notice and appreciate this feeling. Take a few breaths into it.
- Draw golden light in from above your head and send it to the open, pleasurable areas. Let those good feelings expand into the tight or challenged places as you breathe, as if to connect the two with the light.
- Feel free to move and vocalize as you invite this energy to move and harmonize.
- Create a golden sun above you, and with it, draw your energy back from wherever it's been.
- Then, receive the sunlight into your whole body and being. Let the golden rays bring a feeling of love and bliss to all your organs, glands, cells and parts of you.
- Slowly—when you're ready—stretch, open your eyes, and come out of meditation.

ENERGY MOVES FASTER THAN PHYSICAL REALITY

It's both a gift and a challenge to sense energy beyond what our physical senses can see, feel or hear. Knowing how someone is feeling even if they don't admit it, having future events spontaneously flash into your mind, or engaging in conversations in your head are all examples of this. These experiences can be fascinating, and it's often quite helpful to have a heads-up about things! Meanwhile, the contrast between our spiritual visions and 3-D reality can be frustrating and bewildering. To find peace, we need to simultaneously recognize both the instant manifestation of spirit and the slower pace of the mind, emotions and body.

Spirit is infinite, free of the bounds of time and space. When we decide or intend something, or give or receive energy healing, it is done immediately. No process needs to happen. However, if the healing or intention relates to anything beyond the realm of vibration, there is a time lag before physical reality reflects the shift. In this time, we can feel confused or crazy, and doubts and fears may creep in. Common thoughts are: "I thought I had healed this" or "I felt like it was going to happen… but why aren't things going the way I thought?"

Spiritual energy transforms immediately, then the mind does its best to catch up. Next, the emotions need to process until, finally, material reality changes. Understanding this cycle makes change more comfortable and psychic abilities less confounding. Often when you see something, you're right; it's just that now life needs to rearrange itself. The more you can keep your mind, emotions and body fluid and clear, the faster things can happen because there will be less "drag" in the process.

Occasionally, someone or something will have a potential they just don't choose. Therefore, it *is* possible that energy will not manifest into material form. Certain folks are more willing to divide themselves between how they feel and what they do. Some are more ok with a bigger gap between the "real world" and their desired life. Some resist change and others tend to rush. Personally, I process quickly and like things unified, which means I get inpatient with incongruence! We are all humans requiring compassion, and everyone has a right to do it their way.

On this note, another common pitfall of spiritual awareness is that you can get so attached to your vision that you ignore reality. This could mean believing in someone's potential while you fail to address the painful reality of now, or neglecting your own money, health or other important matters because your feet aren't on the ground. Unfortunately, ignoring reality will *not* make it change faster!

The following meditation exercise will support you in harmonizing spirit, body and everything in-between. Now, think of something you're confused about because energy and reality don't seem to be lining up.

MEDITATION: GAUGING A SPECIFIC SITUATION

- Find a comfortable meditation position with your feet flat on the floor.
- Notice your breathing, and then soften and ground on your exhale as you sit taller on the inhale.
- Consider something or someone that you have a vision about. Pick a situation where your vision doesn't quite line up with what's "actually" happening.
- In your mind's eye, imagine a gauge a few feet out in front of you. See a dial or digital display from 0 to 100%, and let it be at 0 or blank for now.
- Ask yourself: Relative to the spiritual truth of this situation, how much does the mind match that truth? This could be your mind, or the mind of anyone involved. Notice the number displayed on the gauge.
- Next, let the gauge reset. Now ask: Given the spiritual truth, how much are the emotions in alignment? See what the gauge shows you.
- Reset the gauge. And finally, ask how much the physical reality is reflecting your spiritual vision *right now*. And observe what percentage that is. Then, dissolve the gauge in your mind's eye.
- If you'd like to ask any other questions, like how long this will take or what you can do in the meantime, please do. Be open to insight that will assist you in creating greater harmony and finding peace in the process.
- When you're complete, bring your attention back to your body and open your eyes.

OWNING YOUR TRUTH

If you often feel confused, out of sorts, disconnected, or stuck on how things "should" be—your connection with your truth may need attention. Your truth is soft yet clear. It is possible to feel simultaneously open and expanded *and* certain in your own guidance. When you don't question what you know, you relax and are naturally open to new information. Paradoxically, living in a spiritual fog can make us averse to taking in new input or resistant to healthy authority.

Most of us have been taught all our lives to look elsewhere for truth. Schools, churches and media do a good job at telling us what to believe. If you're lucky, you had parents or mentors who taught you to look within for answers, but most of us didn't. In most cases, they just didn't know how to—they weren't taught either. And so, they probably modeled to you lots of ways to look outside yourself for truth.

Besides people who mean well, there are those who purposely want authority over others. In fact, sometimes the well-meaning ones are the same people as the authority-seeking folks. Loved ones, teachers or healers may have a need to be validated or to feel close, and so may place subtle controls over your truth. Some are not-so-subtle, and really want to be right or have their way! Those who don't know you, such as marketing companies, have blatant agendas. Many of these can be surprisingly manipulative, and so you'll want to stay in close touch with your own truth so that you don't get swayed.

How do you know if you're in your truth? Remember, it's not rigid. Being rigid implies you're giving too much power to the external world, and then you're in a weak position. Your truth is inarguable. Because you are clear, you have no need to fight, defend or resist. In fact, you may be curious to learn about other perspectives. This is because clarity creates a sense of spaciousness that you don't have when you're confused. Can you recall times you felt this way?

The next exercise is for you to explore how you've given your authority away to others as well as times you've owned your own truth.

There is power in awareness!

WRITING EXERCISE: HAVE YOU BEEN HONORING YOUR TRUTH?

1. To whom in your life have you given seniority over your truth? Who—consciously or not—has tried to program or influence you? Examples may be family, teachers, church, intimate partners, doctors, or a particular community or culture.

2. When in your life have you felt balanced and connected to your truth and higher self?

PSYCHIC PROTECTION

In the past, I learned various psychic protection techniques. Over the years, I used them less and less as I became more present. My #1 recommendation for protecting your energy field is to fill it up with yourself. That said, if that's not so easy right now or for the times when you need extra support, I'd like to offer some practices. Each of the following may work best for certain people or circumstances, so play with them and observe the results you get for yourself.

Protection Roses

In classes, I'll sometimes offer this as a bit of a theater exercise. One person will "vent" about something for a few minutes, and the other will notice how they feel. After taking a few breaths to re-set, the listener then creates a large, fluffy rose a few feet out in front of their body. With this in place, their partner vents again, and the listener notices how they feel. Is there any difference with and without the rose?

Most people express that they are able to listen longer with the rose in front of them. They stay more centered and feel less emotional charge. Even though the rose is in some ways a barrier, many have reported feeling increased closeness to the speaker while it's there. They say they hear more and feel more compassion than they did without the rose. This is interesting, coming out of an era of codependence, and it's very empowering for empaths! The rose is an ancient symbol of being unique and yet part of the whole. It is a great reminder that you can "have your own space" and at the same time connect deeply with others.

You don't need to invite someone to spew their drama so you can learn this technique. However, next time you're going into a situation where you're feeling sensitive, try it. This could be a family dinner, a work meeting or a party. It's great when going out in a crowd, or if you're a teacher or performer or in a position where eyes are on you.

To use the rose, simply imagine it floating a few feet out in front of you, in full bloom and facing away. Stay in your body and notice your space in relationship to it. The rose is like a decoy, so if someone sends energy your way, it will go into the rose before it gets to you.

At the end of your day or when you feel ready, dissolve the rose and let the energy it held go back where it came from. Then, if you wish, create a new rose.

You might explore placing one rose in back of you, as well as one in front. Or, put the rose in front of your head or behind your tailbone or wherever you sense you most need it. Don't get too carried away though, because a fortress of roses will put you in "defense" mode. Have faith that your roses work, and keep your focus on your own energy and life.

Body of Glass

In the midst of intense energy, another great strategy is to pretend you are a "body of glass." Rather than creating a buffer between you and the outside world, just allow any external energy to pass through you without sticking. Imagine your body as fluid light or clear glass, and don't take the world so seriously.

Transmutation

Energy is just… energy. Whatever someone throws your way is a gift. Jealousy is a compliment. Invalidation supports you in honoring yourself. That person who needs you reminds you that you have something.

As with all things intuitive, playfulness and creativity are your allies. What would you like more of? Decide that any energy directed at you turns into that. For example, every judgement becomes a $100 bill. Any criticism just strengthens your grounding cord. Every smidgen of admiration makes you more magnetic to your beloved.

Who cares if that's what they meant? Once it's in your jurisdiction, energy is yours to use as you wish.

Don't fight it all. Turn it into something!

Permission

We are all infinite, but we forget. Projecting our energy outside ourselves is evidence of this. Learning to call your energy back and looking closely at your toxic patterns are great paths back to remembrance.

You can help others remember while also helping yourself through this next technique: *giving permission*. This doesn't need to be out loud; in fact, mostly it's not. The next time that repeat visitor invades your space, simply send them a psychic message that they can have whatever they seek in you. Here, you're showing them that they don't need *you* in order to have it. One way to do this is to imagine tossing them a rose, symbolizing permission to have what they desire.

Truthfully, you don't have their answers; they do. Any good thing they spot in you means it's available for them too. The Universe is infinite! So, gently show your psychic visitors the door. Beyond that, show them a golden road of light back to their own path, where whatever is meant for them awaits.

MEDITATION: SETTING THE ENERGY IN YOUR HOME OR SPACE

The following meditation brings blessings to your home, workplace or any space you choose. For the places you spend most of your time, this is great to do for ongoing psychic protection. It is also useful when going into an important meeting or event, or when you wish to heal or support a loved one in a certain place. For instance, use this for your children's school or when a friend is in the hospital. I also recommend setting the energy for any room where you meditate or give readings.

- Snuggle into your seat, sit tall, and place your feet on the floor as you close your eyes.
- Create your grounding cord and allow yourself to release energy from your body to the center of the earth.
- Find the center of your head and take a seat behind your eyes.
- Now, think of the physical room you're in. Imagine placing gold sticky roses in every corner of the room, top and bottom. These roses will cleanse and uplift the energy in the space.
- Take the corners of the room, and then create a grounding cord from these points down to the center of the earth. Let the room release energy that's stuck or not helpful.
- If you wish, repeat for your entire home or building, along with a workplace or any other places you choose! You could even create a big energy bubble around an outdoor space, and ground that bubble.
- When you feel complete, fill yourself in with gold suns and open your eyes. Enjoy how your space feels!

SPIRITUAL SOVEREIGNTY

You are one with the Divine. You have first dibs on your space. Nothing can come in without your consent, and you are 100% responsible for you. Likewise, other people are 100% responsible for themselves. Isn't that a relief?

Even if it doesn't always seem this way, living "as if" it is true will get you there. Once you assume this is so, you don't blame. You look for your part in things, and you look for what you can do better. You stop asking outside yourself for answers, and you free yourself from the endless loops that limit you. Difficult situations or thoughts or feelings still occur, but they no longer control you, because you know you are free inside. You are curious and creative and resilient.

You are love, and love is allowing. Because of this, finding your sovereignty makes you more open to others, not less. Some people fear or judge the idea of "separating" from loved ones or community, but sovereignty naturally leads to unity. Unity without sovereignty, however, is sticky and false.

Chapter 4:
ENERGETIC ANATOMY

WHAT IS THE ENERGETIC ANATOMY?

Just like our body has organs, glands, blood vessels and nerves, our "energy body" consists of chakras, the aura, energy channels and more. This energy body interfaces with the physical body, and its functions work together with the body's functions. Next, we'll explore each of their purposes, and how to become more aware of these parts of ourselves as well as how to keep them balanced.

THE MEANINGS OF DIFFERENT COLORS

As you awaken to the world of psychic energy, one quick hack is to use color. Almost everyone can start to read quickly this way. Think of a good friend. Then, close your eyes and picture a color that represents this person. If you can do this, you're psychic! Next, ask what that color means to you. Is it indicating something about your friend's personality, or simply how they are doing in this moment? Be open to guidance on this question.

There are no hard and fast rules about what each color means. I suggest trusting your instincts and approaching each reading or meditation with fresh eyes. You might have general associations, yet I suggest being open to what you feel, case by case. While in one instance blue might mean peace and spaciousness, in another it may show up with regimentation, order and uniforms. A milky pinkish white could describe a toxic feminine guilt trip, while a clear rosy pink may illustrate the healthy budding of new love. The expansion of sunny, happy yellow turns into anxiety or distraction in certain cases. So consider the context and use all your senses in interpreting different hues.

Every color has its beauty and healing properties. Remember, when you see a color that's clear and luminous—even if it's dark—it indicates healthy energy. Muddy tones represent stagnation—or energy that's out of place. Your dormant creativity or someone else's energy in your field are examples where muddy tones could show up.

For reference, here are some common associations with various colors:

- **Red:** Anger, action, assertiveness, passion
- **Orange:** Creativity, sexuality, innovation, playfulness
- **Yellow:** Mental energy, optimism, distraction, fear
- **Green:** Healing or growth on any level. Health, money, creative projects, nature or personal transformation
- **Blue:** Peace, calm, clarity, sadness
- **Purple:** Spirituality, royalty, divine feminine transformation
- **Pink:** Love, femininity, romance, sweetness

- **Gold:** The highest vibration in the material realm. Use it to create sacred space or protection.
- **White:** Expansion and transcendence, unconsciousness. I often see white when unconscious energy is releasing out of someone's space. I don't recommend surrounding yourself with white for everyday activities since it can make you ungrounded or overly open to outside energies.
- **Brown / black/ grey:** You'll often see these shades representing foreign or toxic energy that you or others are releasing. They may have other meanings, but this is mostly what I observe.

Besides reading energy by interpreting colors, you can also use them to heal yourself and to manifest your desires. People respond to your vibration as much as your clothes. You would dress differently for a business meeting versus a day at the beach versus a romantic dinner, wouldn't you? Just like that, you can decide what colors to surround yourself with, and you'll find your experience changes accordingly.

CHAKRAS: DISCOVERING THE ENERGY CENTERS

Have you ever seen those images of a person with seven colored flowers like a rainbow going up the spine? Those flowers are chakras. Generally, a red flower is depicted at the tailbone, on up to a violet flower at the crown of the head. Each chakra is an energetic center.

Chakra means "wheel" in Sanskrit, and ancient seers saw these as energetic centers in humans. I think of them as sending and receiving stations. Each one is an important part of our spiritual anatomy, just like organs and glands play a role in our physical anatomy.

I see a variety of colors in each chakra, and do not believe that the root *has* to be red, for instance. No matter what the color—if it's clear and things feel fluid, I believe the color reflects the person's own energy and that it's serving a purpose.

Besides the seven energy centers along the spine, we have minor chakras at the feet and hands. We also have chakras eight to twelve above the head, which have more spiritual functions.

For now, let's explore the seven major chakras one by one:

1st / Root Chakra

The First Chakra is located at the base of the spine, just below the tailbone. Its function is self-preservation. When this chakra is in balance, we feel secure on every level and are fully present in the body. Imbalances here can reflect challenges with health, finances, home—or even emotions or energy that disrupt our sense of safety.

Also known as the Root Chakra, this energy center is associated with the color red and with the adrenal glands. Our life force and fight or flight responses reside here.

2nd / Sacral Chakra

The Second Chakra is located in the low belly and low back area, along the spine a few inches below the navel. Emotions, sexuality and creativity are its functions, as well as the intuitive ability of clairsentience (clear feeling). As compared to the heart's empathy and compassion, feelings in the second chakra are pure and unfiltered. A sense of self-worth, appropriate ownership of your needs, fluidity, pleasure and playfulness indicate balance here. Signs of imbalance include emotional storms, confusion, addiction, entitlement, guilt, shame, manipulation, repressed or excess sexual energy, and creative blocks.

Also knows as the Sacral Center, this chakra is associated with the color orange and with the ovaries or testicles.

3rd / Solar Plexus Chakra

The Third Chakra is located along the spine at the diaphragm and mid-back. Often considered a "power" center, I see its function as that of energy management and distribution. Just as we need good physical digestion to have energy in our bodies, managing our life well requires skill in processing all the input in our environment. Healthy boundaries, a balanced will, and the ability to let go and decompress are signs of a properly functioning third chakra. When this center is out of balance, we may experience overwhelm, power battles, too much arrogance or humility, weak will, competition or an unhealthy need to control (within ourselves or with others).

Also knows as the Solar Plexus Center, this chakra is associated with the color yellow and with the pancreas. Digestive enzymes, blood sugar and our sense of self are all connected with the third chakra.

4th / Heart Chakra

The Fourth Chakra is located in the middle of the chest. Love of self and others, our values, as well as empathy and compassion reside here. When this center is balanced, we are able to give and receive love, and live a life that feels meaningful. Depression, heartache, relationship challenges or lacking a sense of purpose are indications that your heart chakra needs more TLC.

This center is associated with the color green and with the thymus gland. As this gland is key to the immune system, it's a reminder that our relationships and sense of connection in life play a paramount role in our health.

5th / Throat Chakra

The Fifth Chakra is located at the throat, and it's the center of communication and creative expression, along with the psychic abilities of clairaudience (clear hearing) and telepathy (sending and receiving thoughts). Speaking your truth and freely sharing your unique voice are signs of vitality in this arena. When we have communication challenges, can't hear our intuition, or feel like we are not expressing ourselves—this chakra needs balancing.

Also knows as the Throat Chakra, this center is associated with the color blue and with the thyroid gland, governing metabolism in the body.

6th / Third Eye Chakra

The Sixth Chakra is located in the middle of the head, between the ears and behind the eyes. Here we have our ability to visualize. This chakra also gives us clairvoyance, the ability to see psychically what cannot be seen with the physical eyes. It allows us the gift of abstract intuition, which is our ability to process visual imagery and put the pieces of a story together. When you close your eyes and can't picture something, are over-processing, or feel afraid to see, this center could use some clearing.

Also knows as the Third Eye, this chakra is associated with the color indigo and with the pineal gland. Among other things, this is the gland that regulates the body's response to light and our sleep/wake cycles.

7th / Crown Chakra

Sometimes depicted as a lotus flower pointing upwards, sometimes seen as halo, the Seventh Chakra sits at the top of the head. This is where we connect simultaneously to the Divine as well as our higher self and inner authority. Being clear about your own truth, staying open to guidance, and feeling interconnected with all life are signs of balance here. Not feeling protected, lack of faith, or giving up your seniority to external authority are indicators that this energy center needs support.

Also knows as the Crown Chakra, this chakra is associated with the color violet and with the pituitary (or "master") gland, which regulates hormones and directs many body functions.

MEDITATION: CLEARING YOUR CHAKRAS

- Sit upright in meditation.
- Ground yourself, softening on the exhale and sitting taller on the inhale.
- Envision a flower of light at the base of your spine. This is your first, or root chakra.
- What color is this flower? What do you notice about it?
- Imagine a gold, sticky rose out in front of you.
- Swish this sticky rose through the first chakra—front and back. Intend that the rose absorbs any energy that's blocking yours or that does not belong to you.
- As this occurs, be aware of any imagery or messages that you receive.
- Repeat this cleansing process with each chakra all the way up to the sixth. Check both the front and the back of each chakra. We often need clearing in the back because that's where energy gets forgotten or hidden, so to speak.
- When you're ready to balance the seventh, or crown, chakra, please note that this lotus flower points upwards to the sky. Alternately, you may see it as a halo.
- After you've cleared all the chakras, send your gold sticky rose down your grounding cord for some cosmic recycling!
- Lastly, fill yourself in with a gold sun, and come on out of meditation.

THE AURA AND AURA LAYERS

The aura is the electromagnetic field around the body. We can all feel it; often we think of it as getting a vibe from someone. When you're in line at the store and you sense someone pushing behind you… that's your aura feeling theirs! On the other hand, you might meet someone and immediately experience them as warm or cold without real reason. That, too, is you sensing their energetic field.

The aura has seven layers. Each layer corresponds to a chakra, from the closest layer to the body which reflects the first / root chakra to the farthest layer out from the body which reflects the seventh / crown chakra. The energy we see in each layer represents what's going on in the corresponding chakra, and it refers to that area of the person's life. For example, the fourth layer reflects what's going on in the heart. Here, you'll see how someone gives and receives love and empathy, how they share their purpose and passion, and what they value.

The aura changes like the weather, and we can balance it through awareness. Opinions vary, and in my experience, a healthy energy field is usually two to three feet out from the body in every direction—above, below, left, right, front and back—like a body-shaped bubble of colored light. When it doesn't look like that, here's what I see most frequently:

- **The aura is bigger around the top and front**, and less apparent around the lower body and back. Our culture is very forward focused, and we tend to live in our heads. By bringing more energy around our legs and backs, we tend to relax and ground.
- **The energy field is small, less than two feet around the body**. Often this indicates pain, illness or the tendency to pull in. While sometimes appropriate, more often it creates a sense of tightness or contraction that makes one's discomfort worse.
- **Rips, tears or "whacks."** Negative energy from the environment, such as other people's judgements, can damage the aura. This is fixable, but worth noting.
- **The aura is very large**. There are a few cases where this is appropriate,

such as when one is performing or teaching. For instance, I had a conductor client whose energy projected strongly outside himself. He needed to be able to feel the orchestra to do his job! On an ongoing basis, an aura that extends more than five to six feet around the body can create a feeling of overwhelm or being spacey. Every personality is unique, but if you tend to feel "overextended," this is something to check.

Recognizing that your energy extends beyond your physical body explains why some things can't be fixed by physical means alone. If you feel "off," look beyond what you ate and how you slept. Consider that this unease could be due to someone else's emotions sitting in your field, or because your energy is with that person who causes you anxiety instead of inhabiting your own body! Daily energy balancing can help keep this in check.

PRACTICE: SENSING ANOTHER PERSON'S AURA

- Pick someone with whom you can meet in person. Start standing about six feet apart and then rub your own hands together until you feel a little tingle between your palms.
- Next, walk slowly towards your partner with your palms outstretched until you sense a change in sensation. This is their aura! Take your hands in front and behind, to the left and the right, and above and below. Is the aura bigger or smaller in certain places? Warmer or cooler? Are there any dents, empty sections, or areas with excess "charge?" Share what you notice.
- Next, if you wish, switch roles and let your friend feel your aura. As they do, invite them to share what they perceive.

MEDITATION: SETTING YOUR SPACE USING COLOR

- Sit and relax with your spine straight and feet flat on the floor.
- Observe your grounding cord connecting your hips to the center of the earth.
- As you exhale, consciously soften and let go of any tension in your body. Sit taller on your inhale and—with ease—feel the fullness in your heart, diaphragm and belly.
- Imagine a body-shaped bubble around you.
- In your mind's eye, observe what your bubble looks and feels like. Is it even around your body? How large is it? Do you see colors or dark or light spots? Does it seem like there are any rips or tears?
- Given what you noticed, what does this mean to you?
- Now, balance your aura using your powers of visualization. See it two to three feet out around your body in every direction—above, below, left, right, in front and in back. Smooth out the edges, fill in the gaps, and tuck it into your grounding cord so it can release what no longer serves you.
- Invite in a desire you have for the rest of your day or evening. What color makes you feel the way you'd like to feel?
- Next, see your aura flooded with your chosen color. Enjoy surrounding yourself with that color and all the feelings and qualities it represents. You'll go back to your day radiating and attracting these qualities. You can change the color at any time, based on what you need in that moment.
- When you're ready, envision a big golden sun above your head and let it magnetize your own energy back to you.
- Drink in the golden light from above into every part of you. You'll still keep the color you chose, knowing it's now illuminated by this light.
- Enjoy receiving this light as long as you like, and then come out of meditation.

COSMIC AND EARTH ENERGY CHANNELS

Your energy body is in constant connection with your environment. Allowing healthy energy to flow through you is part of how you keep your field clear! Choosing to receive healing energy from both the earth and cosmos is one way to do this. We have built-in energy channels for these purposes.

Here they are:

Earth Energy Channels

Beginning in the soles of each foot, our earth channels go up through each leg, through the hips and into the root chakra. From here, the earth energy flows down the grounding cord.

Ideally, our feet chakras are always open and drawing in healing energy from the earth. In practice, many of us live from the waist or neck up, and we'd benefit from putting our feet on the ground and using our legs more often to keep these channels open.

Cosmic Energy Channels

Cosmic energy cascades down from above into two channels at the back of the head. These two channels branch into four channels at the base of the neck, and they run all the way down the back of the spine. They flow through each of the seven major chakras and into the grounding cord. After mixing with the earth energy, your cosmic energy goes back up the spine, cleansing the front of each chakra. It then washes through the aura as it showers out from the top of the head and hands.

Just like earth energy, the cosmic energy will continually pour in and cycle through as an automatic loop. All you have to do is be open to it.

Next, I'll lead you in a meditation so you can turn on your earth and cosmic energy at will.

MEDITATION: RUNNING EARTH AND COSMIC ENERGY

- Sit with your feet flat on the floor and spine upright.
- Close your eyes, breathe and relax.
- Say hello to your grounding cord. If you have a grounding cord from before, great! See if it needs strengthening, clearing, reattaching or any other updates. If not, create a brand-new waterfall, tree trunk or whatever kind of grounding cord feels right for you at this time.
- Feel your feet, and then rub them on the floor until you feel a tingly sensation in the soles of each foot. In doing this, you are waking up your feet chakras! Remove your shoes if you prefer, but it's not necessary.
- Next, imagine drawing in the most healing earth energy you can imagine. What color is it? Choose any color in the rainbow, and perhaps get a sense of where within the earth this is coming from. What are its qualities?
- Invite this colored light to flow up each leg channel, through the knees and hips, then flushing through the root chakra and down your grounding cord. This light is healing to all the spaces it touches.
- Once you've opened up to it, this earth energy will continue as an ongoing loop. You can always play with the speed or color, or with the size of your channels. Once you've got it flowing, however, it will continue without your attention.
- Next, look upwards in your mind's eye, and picture a beautiful light flowing down through the top of your head. Choose any color except white, brown, black or grey. Notice what color feels inspiring!
- Let this colored light pour down through the two cosmic channels along the back of your head, branching into four channels along your spine and clearing each chakra along the way.
- As these streams of light reach your tailbone, allow your cosmic energy to mingle with the earth energy that's coming up the legs.
- Imagine a mixture of about 10-20% earth energy and 80-90% cosmic energy and see this flowing up the front of the spine in two

channels—left and right. Any excess energy at your root goes down your grounding cord.
- This upward-flowing energy mixture will clear each chakra from the front side. It makes a luminous shower of light out the top of your head. Let this wash through your entire aura and down your grounding cord. As you do this, you cleanse your entire field.
- Meanwhile, as the light moving upwards reaches your heart and throat, see smaller streams of it branching off to flow down your arms and out your hands. You have little mini showers of light now coming off your palms.
- Just like the earth energy, your cosmic energy will continue to flow once you've activated it. You can check it once a day or as needed. Play with widening or narrowing the channels, changing the color or speed, and see what works best for you.
- Enjoy this as long as you'd like. Before you come out of meditation, create a gold sun above your head. Let it flood your body and aura with your own creative power, replenishing anything you released with light.

THE CREATIVE RINGS

Above your physical head are three creative rings, which look like halos. I typically see them spaced about a foot apart, starting about a foot higher than the crown chakra. As you get into more advanced energy healing and manifesting, these rings are great to know about and work with. They are not often discussed as part of the energetic anatomy, and I have discovered them through advanced psychic trainings along with my own meditation. Clearing and balancing them has proven to be highly impactful!

Why are these creative rings so important? They relate to how we manifest everything in our lives as well as how we, ourselves, incarnate into form. As I see it, incarnation is continuous, and not just a one-time event. Based on the state of our energy and consciousness, we are always creating.

In the process of creation, there are three cycles— (1) create, (2) destroy and (3) maintain. These are Universal, and many spiritual traditions reference them. Christianity speaks of the Father, the Son and the Holy Ghost. Hindu deities include Brahma (create), Shiva (destroy) and Vishnu (preserve). There is a time for new beginnings, a time for taking care of what we have, and a time for letting go. The creative rings each pertain to one of these aspects.

Closest to the body and crown chakra, the first creative ring governs maintaining. How do you care for your life and what you have? This includes how you as a spirit enter the medium of your body and take form. We will cover this later in more depth.

In the middle is the "destroy" ring, which pertains to how you handle transformation and letting go. We must be able to let go if we are going to create anything, yet there are more and less beneficial ways to do this. At best, this is the aspect of Divine transformation.

At the top is the "create" ring, and I have always seen this ring as a symbol of one's true self. What is your soul's unique expression? Find it here.

Most of us tend to favor one or more aspects of creation over the other(s). What are your tendencies? Do you prefer to create, destroy or maintain? Is there any aspect you avoid? In the following meditation, you'll take a closer look and learn to balance your creative rings.

MEDITATION: BALANCING YOUR CREATIVE RINGS

- Relax and sit tall with your feet flat on the floor.
- Ground yourself and check in with your body and breathing.
- Bring your awareness to the center of your head. Find your sanctuary space there, and be aware of being an infinite being, witnessing life.
- In your mind's eye, look up through the crown of your head and get a sense of three additional halos above your body.
- Are these rings balanced or lopsided? Adjust them as needed. Be sure they sit evenly and that there is plenty of space in-between them.
- What color is each one? There are no right or wrong colors, however please notice: Are the colors clear or are there dark spots or energies that don't seem to belong?
- If you see colors or energies that don't look right or feel natural, imagine a gold sticky rose and use it to "dust" off your creative rings. Allow the rose to absorb anything that doesn't belong so that your rings begin to shine again.
- Next, clear out the spaces in-between your rings. This will help your creative aspects work together harmoniously.
- When you're done clearing, send your gold sticky rose down your grounding cord.
- With repeated practice, you may notice that one—or more—of your rings tends to need regular clearing, and one or more does not. You may sense gunk in the space between two of them, or between the lowest ring and your crown chakra. Whatever you see frequently indicates a pattern you are working on, and with time and attention, you can heal it.
- Create a giant golden sun above your head. Let this sun magnetize all the love, light and creative power you have left with other people and places, through all points in time. Bring in this sunlight and allow it to fill all parts of your body and energy body.

Chapter 5:
USING INTUITION FOR YOURSELF

THE POWER OF INTENTION

Your psychic abilities don't exist in a vacuum. The world of energy is less black and white, and more like poetry. Of course, certain facts are inarguable, yet whatever you bring to a scenario will color how you experience it.

Depending on your state of consciousness, the same person might seem either pushy or energetic. Moving through that challenge at work could feel either gratifying or punishing. Look out at a landscape through a green lens and then a purple one, and you'll see a different scene each time.

Based on the assumptions you have when you look, varying things could seem true. It reminds us to be flexible around right and wrong, good and bad. We understand more when we ask, "According to what person?" or "Within what context?" As we answer these questions, we realize the validity of different perspectives.

This awareness grows compassion. It reminds you of the freedom you have inside, and it helps those around you, whether professionally or just in your own life. One of my favorite prompts in reading energy is "Tell me more about that." I don't necessarily ask my client to talk more; this is something I say internally as I'm receiving impressions during the reading. It is a spiritual practice—in that I set aside my personal beliefs and feelings and get curious about someone else. I learn a lot this way, and it helps me to be of most service.

When it comes to getting answers for yourself, having a curious attitude also brings more fruitful outcomes. As Einstein said, "Problems cannot be solved with the same mindset that created them." And so, when you're feeling stuck, your intention could be to expand your perspective so you can see what you're not seeing. This is where going out on a walk or talking with someone outside your situation can provide a much-needed shift in your energy. Simply feeling different about something can create a new outcome! For example, if you notice your internal script saying, "I'm trapped… it's complicated…" over and over, your new mantra could be "I am now finding easy solutions to my situation, and I feel empowered." You might feel inauthentic at first, yet simply thinking these new thoughts will start to open new doors.

Become bigger. If you were to pour a handful a salt into a glass of water and then take a sip, the salty taste would dominate. Drop that same handful of salt into a lake, take a drink, and the salt is unnoticeable. Consider that the salt is your problems, and then be the lake. Stretching yourself in this way can mean setting an intention even if—*especially if*— you have no idea how you'll realize it. This will invite support as you affirm the vastness of your soul as well as the Universe's infinite creativity. Giving more attention to what you intend can make problems shrink, simply due to lack of attention.

When reading others or just going about your day, having an intention offers you a layer of psychic protection. I recommend trying this before going to work, falling asleep, or making that important phone call. Sometimes my daughter asks me on the way to school if we can set intentions for her day. It takes one minute.

Having an intention means you are present, which implicitly protects you from energies that aren't yours. Simply finding your own personal balance before you face a challenging subject helps a lot. Further, deciding to be amused means things won't get too serious. Choosing to feel confident protects you from sabotage, and it minimizes doubts.

Getting what you want in life requires finding a balance between letting things happen and directing the outcome. Making the most of your psychic readings is no different. I tell my clients to come to their session with a few specific questions, but also to be open to what arises.

Each day *is* like a trip through Best Buy. There is so much you could possibly pay attention to in any moment, so you need to go in knowing what you want! Likewise, once you realize all the energy there is to experience, you'll want to be discerning. This is a practice in and of itself. Continually, you put out intention simply through your thoughts, feelings and choices. And so, intention not only determines how you do psychic readings, it also dramatically influences your life.

HOW TO ASK GOOD QUESTIONS

Ask and you shall receive. So, if you ask, "Is he cheating on me?" the best you will get is that answer. Whether it's yes or no, the fact that you're asking that question indicates a level of unease. What if you could clear that up?

Years ago, a client asked me, "Am I going to get a promotion?" I had just met this young man, and so I had no idea what he did, but I felt a sense of compression and boxed-in thinking when he asked me that question.

"You don't like your job, do you?" I replied.

"No," he admitted.

"What do you do?"

"I'm a mechanic."

Huh, I thought. This guy felt more artistic, and his energy got flat talking about his job. I saw a lot of bright mental energy representing his soul, and I shared this with him.

As we explored, it turned out that he came from a family of mechanics. It hadn't even occurred to him that he would earn money another way, even though he was unhappy!

We did a healing to clear the programming that he "had" to work on cars, and then energized his dream of creating video games. I gave him a reading on how to move forward and showed him it was possible.

Unlike some psychics who will just give you answers, I like to guide you to find your questions. Unlike some who will just tell you what you want to hear, I prefer to see what that is, and then describe pathways to get there. Telling you it's going to happen when you're actually stuck in a pattern preventing it is not honest or helpful. Giving you bad news, even if honest, doesn't feel like enough. Answering your yes and no, A or B questions can shine some light if I explain pros and cons of each. Yet we could take it further and see if there's a better way to realize your deeper desires.

Good questions are like intentions. You are already asking yourself questions all day long, based on where you place your awareness. If you're wondering if you're going to get sick, or if you can trust a certain person—you'll be more likely to fall ill or hear lies. Rather, notice your fears and doubts, and then consider what it would look like if things went way better than you imagined. What would you like instead of the thing you are fearing? And then, wonder about how you could participate in attracting that.

Whatever we assume will also color our questions. For example, if you're focused on immediate results, you might get irritated and desperate to fix something because you're "in the moment." Thinking long-term about the same situation might change the questions you ask about it.

Following are two exercises to help you stretch yourself and ask more fulfilling questions.

WRITING EXERCISE: DISCOVERING YOUR QUESTIONS

If you could ask anything right now of a psychic or wise guide, what would you ask? Don't censor yourself. Think about your "burning questions" and let go of trying to be your most enlightened self for a moment.

1.

2.

3.

4.

5.

For each of your questions 1-5, what are you hoping to get out of the answer? For example, if you asked, "What does my co-worker think of me?" your deeper desire might be to feel approval or harmony at work, or to heal a challenging pattern you have with certain types of people. Please translate this to your circumstances and write down the motivation behind each of your questions.

1.

2.

3.

4.

5.

Considering what you are wanting out of the answers, are your initial questions the best questions you can ask? If not, write your new questions below. For example: "How can I learn to speak up when I encounter domineering personalities?" or "Why am I needing approval from certain people?" or "How could I show up at work to help create a harmonious atmosphere where my light shines bright?"

1.

2.

3.

4.

5.

NEUTRALITY

Neutrality is your surprise ticket to freedom. People think of it as cold nothingness, when in fact it's a highly dynamic way of being. In this state, you can still have preferences, and you probably will. However, once in it, it's likely you'll just witness things that would have otherwise triggered you. You won't be hooked by desire or aversion. All your emotions become accessible, and this feels both easier and more nourishing. You've taken all expectations off of the feelings, and so they are what they are. Your experience is refreshingly pure.

Just being neutral where someone else is not gives them a healing. We are resonant beings, and they cannot stay trapped when you are free right next to them! So, it doesn't matter whether you're giving them a reading, having a coffee, or sitting next to them on an airplane. This is also why the greater amount of light you embody, the more those who resist healing stay away from you. Years ago, a neighbor used to pick fights with me right when I came home from spiritual seminars. It was never at any other time, which was comical. Apparently, my evolution did not make her comfortable.

If we are not neutral in our own lives, we end up chasing some things and avoiding others. Once we realize that this doesn't make us as happy as we'd hoped, the merits of neutrality become quite obvious.

My teacher illustrated this with a story of a reading he did for an obese woman in Hollywood. When she asked why she couldn't seem to lose weight, he saw a past life where she'd been starving. Then in a culture where extra weight was deemed attractive, she had prayed and prayed, "Please God, make me fat!" Fast forward hundreds of years to Los Angeles, and she got the large body she'd asked for. Oops! "Please God, make me thin!" was her new plea. We humans do this type of pendulum-swing so much, always chasing something "out there." What will it take to speed up the arrival of true happiness?

For me, being a professional intuitive and healer has increased my spiritual freedom exponentially. In part, this is due to my practice of neutrality. When I'm working, I focus on service and my judgement has no place. That does not mean I will support anything unethical that's causing harm. However, most humans are well-intended and just have blind spots. We fumble, we get stuck, and we need someone to hold our hand and shine the light. That I can do. It's not about me when I read you. I can see you clearer perhaps than I see me, and yet bearing witness to your reality opens up mine.

It works both ways. Your neutrality helps you read and heal others, and reading others dissolves your attachments.

MEDITATION: FINDING NEUTRALITY AND INNER FREEDOM

This is one of my favorite meditations! It's kind of a "catch all" energy clearing. It's a great go-to when you're feeling stuck or "off" and don't know quite what it is or what to do about it.

- Sit in a quiet place with your feet flat on the floor.
- Say hello to your grounding cord, connecting your hips to the center of the earth.
- Allow a long, slow breath out as you send any stress or tension down your grounding cord.
- Center your awareness in a sanctuary space behind your eyes.
- Looking out from there, imagine a bright, fluffy red rose a few feet out in front of you. See that rose in full bloom, and let it absorb any "red" energy that's not serving you. In focusing on this red, you'll also become neutral to any people, feelings or energies that vibrate at that color. Whatever triggers you tends to dissolve when you face it.
- What is your sense about what you're releasing? Maybe that's anger, impatience, desire or something else. You might be clearing energy that says, "I can't have anger" or "I'm always angry." Or you may be letting go of a charge you have around passion, simplicity, or assertiveness— whatever red brings up for you. This could be your energy or someone else's, current or from the past. Likely there are several layers to what you're healing, and you don't have to know what they all are for this exercise to work. Just decide to let the energy go and it will.
- Once your red rose feels complete, watch as it floats off to the edge of the Universe and goes "poof" in a burst of light.
- One by one, repeat this exercise with a rose of each color in the rainbow. Stay behind your eyes and give yourself lots of space in relationship to each rose.
- Notice any body sensations, pictures, feelings or auditory messages you receive as you heal yourself in relationship to each color.

- Be sure to fill in with a gold sun, replenishing thoroughly when you're done. You just did a lot of healing!

CAN YOU LEARN TO PREDICT THE FUTURE?

Sometimes people equate "psychic" with "fortune-teller." This is not my focus and I caution against it for many reasons.

For one, even the best psychics can only read probabilities, because everyone has free will. I don't want to program someone or set them up for disappointment because they're expecting a certain result that doesn't happen.

In addition, jumping ahead to the future can prevent us from going through the processes we need to get there. Even when things are difficult, avoiding what's happening today usually tends to delay a positive future, and it can cause more pain and unconsciousness to build up. It can be hard to stay present sometimes, but it's typically necessary to move through your current lessons before you can get somewhere new.

Here's how this works in practice: A question like "What should I do about my relationship with Bob?" is usually best answered by looking at current dynamics, not by trying to figure out the future. In a case like this, I might use a rose reading, a technique I'll lead you through next, to better understand the situation before giving someone in such a situation advice.

Based only on what someone tells me, it might be easy to say, "Break up," until I look and see a man's heart is sincere despite how he's showing up. An apparently tough situation may be helping my client grow in necessary ways. Knowing the relationship is meant to end may not help if she needs to learn certain lessons first.

Once these deeper layers get revealed, people find freedom. Hard times can be opportunities for empowerment. Knowing what each experience offers allows us to ask, "Is there a healthier way I can grow here?" or "Now that I see the bigger picture, what would I like to do?"

Save for dramatic cases such as abuse, abruptly ending something difficult doesn't tend to work. We generally just repeat the painful scenario with a new person or in a new job, and then scream at God saying, "How could you keep doing this to me?!" Or we beat ourselves up, asking, "What's wrong with me?" Those questions lead nowhere, except to remind us to stop and ask why we're repeating patterns. Our higher selves are ingenious at creating ways to trigger us, if that's what it takes to finally grow.

As you step into reading other people, I encourage you to consider how you can support them on these deeper levels. Egos want answers, but I trust if you're reading this, you want more and so do the people you will help.

Sometimes we cannot see, or we see something and then it changes. When future forecasts prove inaccurate, what happened? Most likely, it was one of these things:

- One or more of the people involved shifted their energy, and thus shifted the outcome.
- You or your client needed to think a certain future was imminent in order to get where you / they needed to go.
- The person making the prediction was ungrounded, unethical or inexperienced at reading and interpreting energy.

I do believe we can see future probabilities if we're meant to, for example if someone needs encouragement or a warning in order to choose the best path. Questions such as "Should I take Path A or B?" will tend to reveal at least some of what's likely on either path. I love giving readings like this because they allow the client free will. I'll paint the picture of how each path looks in the moment, and the client gets to decide which one they'd rather have. If neither path looks good, we can ask if there's a solution they haven't yet thought of. With these types of readings, we receive valuable information about possible road bumps and opportunities along each path, as well as clarity about what the client really wants. With this knowledge, they may find new approaches or subtle adjustments that make their chosen path even better.

Have you ever pictured something "out of the blue" regarding your own life and then it happened? In cases like this, clients have asked me, "Did I manifest it or pick up on this?" It can go either way. It is possible to manifest without "trying," if your soul wants something you aren't consciously thinking about. And the more you practice visualizing and clearing energy, the quicker you'll be able to use mental image pictures to create. It is also possible that you just got a flash of something headed your way.

MEDITATION: ROSE READINGS FOR SPECIFIC AREAS OF YOUR LIFE

- Sit in a meditative space and ground yourself.
- Find your point of awareness in the center of your head.
- Run your earth and cosmic energy, and then balance your aura.
- Now, pick an area of your life that you would like insight on. This could be your love life, your purpose, health, money, a person you know, a project or opportunity, and anything else you choose.
- Allow a rose to appear a few feet out in front of you. This rose can be any color, size or shape. Let it represent the subject of your question in present time. Study the details of this rose.
- Ask yourself, "What does this rose symbolize to me?" For instance, a rose in full bloom may mean that area of your life is blossoming, whereas a bud represents a new beginning. Thorns often represent protection, while leaves may be contracts with others. I was taught that a long stem indicated an old soul, or if the rose represents a situation rather than a person, it could mean that the situation is well-grounded.
- Get curious about this rose's environment along with its specific appearance. How does all this make you feel? If you could make up a story about this area of your life based on what you see in the rose, what would the story say?
- When you feel complete, see this rose dissolve or go "poof" into a burst of light.
- Next, one by one, look at new roses to represent any other areas of your life or topics you choose. Repeat the process above with each rose.
- When you're done, fill in with a gold sun.

ARE YOUR DECISIONS YOUR OWN?

When I started my first year of clairvoyant training, people thought I was learning to be psychic. I would typically groan and say, "It feels more like I'm in therapy." I quickly figured out that being psychic was the easy part. As I discovered that so many thoughts, emotions, desires and choices I'd assumed were my own were not, it was both liberating and uncomfortable. I started to realize who I really was, what I truly felt and believed, and what I actually desired. There was definitely some unraveling of all I had chosen based on other people's truths!

If you'd like to use your intuition for decision-making, please realize it's not just about getting the "right" answer. Unless your main goal is to please everyone around you or to repeat your programming or past, I highly recommend clearing the energy around your choices, so you can make them based on your soul's truth today.

When we have an important choice to make, we often feel fear, desire or doubt, and we come up against beliefs and expectations. While some of this may be true and valuable, the lens we look through is likely influenced by people we know, our environment and the past. Seeing and cleaning up anything tainting this lens will ensure that we make the decisions that are right for us today.

Remember, what's truly yours needs to be worked through, while other people's energy can be simply released. Take your time if you need to process a decision, but don't belabor it because of someone else's agenda.

Note: making decisions based on how things feel is a feminine way. Deciding based on vision and goals is a masculine way. When either part is left out, we can have problems. We all have both inside us, and it may be more helpful to use one or the other at any given moment. If your emotions tend to run the show, you may need to consider practicalities more often. Alternately, if you only base your choices on bullet points and outcomes, you are also missing something important. Try letting both facts and feelings collaborate in your life, and perhaps seek out balanced input from someone you trust, if you know you tend one way.

Next is a meditation to support you in clearer decision-making.

MEDITATION: HOW TO MAKE A DECISION USING YOUR INTUITION

- Sit down in a quiet place, ground and breathe.
- Pick a decision you have to make and consider two potential choices, A and B (knowing there are always more than two).
- Imagine that you have committed to making Choice A. See yourself doing it and feel the feelings as if it were so. Notice what thoughts arise and how your body responds.
- A few feet in front of you, envision a gauge that goes from 0-100%. Ask, "How much of the energy that I'm feeling around this choice is mine?"
- See what percent shows up on the gauge.
- Then, re-set the gauge and ask, "How much of the energy I'm feeling around this choice is in present time?"
- See what percent that is, and then clear and release the gauge.
- In your mind's eye, imagine a rose that represents you making Choice A with 100% commitment. Allow all the thoughts, feelings and energies that aren't yours, aren't current, or aren't helpful to go into the rose. When this feels complete, send the rose off and explode it.
- Repeat this process, beginning with the gauge, for Choice B.
- Next, ask what you really desire now. Open to guidance about good questions to ask as well as anything that will support you in having your desires met.
- Create a gold sun, and bring in the essence of your desire, as if you are having it now. Commit to receiving this or something better.

UNDERSTANDING AND UTILIZING YOUR DREAMS

Each night while your physical body sleeps, you take a spiritual "field trip." Dreams are a potent time to receive information and healing. Many people have had dreams that come true, and this can be an entry point to psychic awareness. The phrase, "I'm going to sleep on it" also points to the clarity we can find through dreams.

What many don't know is that we can choose our dream experiences. Fear of nightmares need not be if we harness this awareness and capacity. The next meditation exercise will offer some healing towards this and other astral experiences.

To begin working with your dreams, I recommend setting intentions when you go to bed at night. If you wait until you're exhausted, this will be harder to do, so be sure to get to bed a little bit earlier than necessary. Then, set your intentions by writing them down, saying them out loud, or meditating and visualizing them. Is there a place you'd like to explore or an event you'd like to prepare for? What about a person you need to speak with, but haven't had the opportunity and courage in waking life? Would you like to have a healing for a current challenge, or support with something you're calling into your life? One of my favorite things is to go to sacred places—spiritual vortexes of sorts—in my dreams! At the very least, you can surround yourself with a favorite color before you go to bed.

If you wake up in the middle of the night with a bad dream, remind yourself that you can change it. Since she was little, I have told my daughter, "Remember, you can do anything you want in your dreams." And she tells me she knows. This is a powerful approach, both before bed and in the wee hours as needed.

In the morning, try to take a few minutes to be aware of your dreams before you get out of bed. Perhaps have a journal to write your insights in, or you might tell a partner or friend. Even if you don't remember the details of your dreams, it's common to wake with a helpful knowing or feeling that you didn't have before bed. You might also have a sense of going somewhere or meeting someone in particular, even though you don't know what happened. Then there is the "déjà vu" you'll find later, when you run into that person you dreamed about!

Have fun with your dreams.

MEDITATION: HEALING YOUR ASTRAL BODY

If you tend towards bad dreams, don't sleep well, or would like to use this potent time for healing and intuitive guidance, this meditation is for you. Since sleep occupies such a huge part of our lives, I highly recommend being more conscious in how you approach it.

- Sit upright for meditation and ground your hips to the center of the earth.
- Rub your feet on the floor, waking up your feet chakras, and run your earth and cosmic energy.
- Find your sanctuary space in the center of your head.
- As you sit in your aura bubble, imagine your astral body a few feet in front of you. This will look similar, yet distinct from the bubble you're sitting in.
- Notice the silver cord in-between your solar plexus, or third chakra, and the third chakra of your astral body. This cord allows you to go on spiritual "field trips" at night and then come back to your body each morning.
- Check the condition of this cord, along with the connecting points at either end. Notice any dark or apparently foreign energy, and any rips or frays. Ask for any insight about what you sense.
- Next, take a gold, sticky rose and flush it through this cord, cleansing it. Reconnect the ends smoothly if necessary. Reclaim this cord and fill it with your own energy.
- As you sit in your physical body, proceed to clear your entire astral body with your gold sticky rose. Make the rose bigger if you need to and remember—there's no time or space in spirit! Let it soak up any energy that's not helping in your dream life.
- When you're done, release your gold sticky rose off to the horizon and see it burst into pure light.
- Think about what you'd like to experience in your dreams. This may be as specific as solving a certain problem or connecting with a loved

one. Or you might choose a quality like "peace" or a color that makes you feel good.
- Put those intentions in a big gold sun and fill your astral body with this light.
- Next, fill your aura and physical body with a gold sun, calling your energy back from wherever it's been besides here and now.
- Finally, draw your astral body towards you to merge with your aura. Alternately, stand up and walk into your astral body, reconnecting your bodies that way.

LIVING IN FLOW

How is it that you're drawn to go to a certain store at a certain time, and then run into a long-lost friend? Why do you keep getting distracted, leave late, and then avoid an accident? When plans don't work out, have you ever noticed that what happens instead answers your prayer?

These are all examples of living in serendipity, of being in flow. I love this space! I'm lucky because I'm an entrepreneur, and I set up my schedule to flow quite a bit. Where you can, I suggest playing with this. Just do what you feel like doing, moment by moment. This is not about being irresponsible or reactive, but rather responsive to the energetic currents you sense. This works best when you center yourself first. So, you might start your day with meditation, and let your instincts guide you from there.

On the days I live in flow, I typically have a list of things I need to do, as well as things I'd like to do. I often look at these lists and see what "lights up." What feels good? Which do I have happy pictures about? Where do I feel an energy drag or see a closed door? Some ideas may be good ideas, just not at that moment. If I need to do something on a certain day, of course, I'll do it. Yet I'll often hear, "Don't call now" and then get a strong hit that it's time just a half an hour later. I am only able to hear those messages when I stay fluid, receptive and present.

Living in flow is a fantastic example of how practical intuition increases your efficiency, happiness and success. In a business coaching program, I learned that one secret of millionaires is having dedicated "focus time." During this time, you are not available to clients, you're not doing business tasks or tending to family and friends. It's not "free time" or personal time, as we think of it. This is time to focus exclusively on your projects, without distraction. My sense is that this time marries the magic of flow with the potency of intention. You can try it with business projects, or just dedicate time to focus on your personal growth or personal goals. Flow and see what happens!

Chapter 6:
TYPES OF INTUITION

QUIZ: WHAT ARE YOUR NATURAL PSYCHIC GIFTS?

Do you often experience any of the following? Please put a checkmark next to each "yes," then see below to assess your results.

1. You know who's on the phone before you pick it up.
2. You call someone and they say, "I was just thinking of you" or "You called at the perfect time."
3. You say something and the person you're talking to says, "I was just thinking of that," or they say something you were just thinking of.
4. You have conversations with people in your head, and they feel real to you.
5. You get mental images of people or situations.
6. You see pictures of events that come true in the future.
7. You see random flashes of light, perhaps when something significant is happening.
8. You see light or color around people, animals or plants.
9. You feel emotions that you don't know why you feel, then discover someone you know has been feeling that way.
10. After touching someone or being near them, you notice your body has taken on their symptoms, pains, food cravings, etc.
11. You experience intuition through body sensations, for example goosebumps, getting warm or tingly, or feeling nauseous.
12. Your body moves in certain directions without you "thinking" about where to go. You feel your body's wisdom in this.
13. You just know things "off the top of your head."
14. You take a test (or perhaps did when you were a child) and just know the answers.
15. You have revelations or sudden big-picture "a-has."
16. You feel connected to the Divine or a sense of higher truth.
17. It feels like you hear your angels or guides giving you messages.
18. You hear music or poetry in your head.
19. You get answers and clarity through writing or journaling.

20. Your intuitive answers come as "random" thoughts, words or phrases.
21. You frequently feel "spaced out."
22. It sometimes feels like you tap into an energy larger than yourself, perhaps in times of creativity or spiritual practice.
23. You crave sugar, caffeine, alcohol or other substances.
24. You tend to be moody and easily triggered, and sometimes you aren't "yourself"—especially when you're not properly nourished and grounded.

ANSWERS: In which sections did you get mostly "yes?" These are your strongest abilities.

- **1-4: Telepathy** (sending and receiving thoughts from person to person)
- **5-8: Clairvoyance** (seeing mental image pictures)
- **9-12: Clairsentience** (feeling things in your body)
- **13-16: Claircognizance** (aka knowingness, the ability to know the big picture or intuit without pictures, feelings, words or sounds)
- **17-20: Clairaudience** (the ability to hear spirit or one's higher self)
- **21-24: Mediumship** (aka trans-mediumship, the ability to enter and leave your physical body and/ or to channel spiritual energy)

Next, we'll dive deeper into each of these abilities and experience them for ourselves!

CLAIRSENTIENCE

Clairsentience is "clear feeling," and it's a second chakra psychic ability. With this sense, your feeling-body receives information and intuitively responds. If you're making love or collaborating on a creative project, clairsentience feels awesome. Not so much if you're a massage therapist working on someone with whiplash! So, as with all our intuitive senses, discernment is key.

The second chakra wants proof that something is real, and so these feelings are palpable. Here are some examples:

- Feeling goose bumps or chills when a powerful truth is spoken
- You move a certain way without thinking about it.
- Knowing which foods or other things your body needs (especially powerful for a woman in pregnancy)
- Feeling restless before an earthquake or when circumstances are unsettled, even if you don't know why
- A father working in his yard felt a sudden pull to run inside, and he ended up saving his young son from getting hurt.
- Gaining information about a situation through physical sensations (warm and fuzzy, nauseous, cool, agitated, etc.)
- Clairsentience causes problems when:
- You take on other people's physical symptoms.
- You feel emotions that aren't yours and try to fix or process them.
- You act on other people's body cravings (sex, food, substances etc.).

If any of the above are happening, that's a sign to clear your second chakra! You can use the bubble technique from Chapter 3 on "Psychic Self-Care," as well as grounding and running cosmic and earth energy. Then, replenish with a gold sun, and be sure to fill in the spaces you cleared out.

MEDITATION: USING YOUR BODY AS A PENDULUM

If you ask, your body will tell you what it likes and doesn't like. Next up is an exercise that will allow you to ask your body about different foods, supplements, cosmetics or anything else you're wondering about.

You may have seen or used a pendulum, typically a crystal or stone hanging from a chain. With a pendulum, you can hold it steady, ask a "yes" or "no" question, and then let go of the stone. Your "yes" might be indicated by the pendulum moving in a circle, back and forth or side to side. Another type of movement would indicate "no" or "maybe."

Using your body as a pendulum is simple! Your body will pull away if it doesn't like something, and it will draw closer when it does. Try it!

Choose at least three items and set them in front of you one at a time. For each, notice if your body pulls forward, backwards or stays neutral in response to the item. This is one way to feel whether a product is good for you or not.

Please note: These readings are "in the moment." A particular food might be good for you, but not at the time you test it. For example, you get a "no" on coffee at 10 pm, but a "yes" at 8 am. Or a certain supplement might be needed temporarily as you heal a specific condition—but it wouldn't be appropriate to take all the time. As you get more savvy, you can ask your body how many days or weeks you should take something, and other specific questions.

You can also ask things like "Body, do you want to go to yoga today?" or "Is this person the right doctor for me?" If you're wondering about an experience and not a "thing" you can set in front of you, write some words about the experience on a piece of paper. For instance, write the name of the doctor or yoga class. Set that piece of paper down in front of you and notice if your body pulls forward, back or stays neutral.

TELEPATHY

Telepathy is your ability to send and receive thoughts. So, when you have a conversation with someone in your head, that's a telepathic experience. If you finish your friend's sentence or she calls and you were just thinking of her, that's a telepathic experience. With awareness, this can be fun and quite useful.

There are two types of telepathy: (1) broad band and (2) narrow band. Narrow band telepathy is with people you know, and often happens in close relationships. Broad band telepathy is with the collective. What are the thoughtforms in your neighborhood, town or city? What are you receiving from the media, social media, or from certain groups or institutions?

When you aren't conscious or don't know how to release all these thoughts and conversations, this can cause a fuzzy head, insomnia, confusion about relationships or even about what you think. Sinus issues may point to challenges with narrow band telepathy, whereas the fifth layer of your aura holds collective mental broadcasts.

Next, I'll share with you a meditation to clear all this telepathic congestion, which I liken to your psychic "voicemail."

MEDITATION: CLEARING YOUR TELEPATHIC CHANNELS

- Sit with your feet flat on the floor, breathe and go within.
- Create your grounding cord.
- Imagine a gold, sticky rose a few feet out in front of you.
- Bring the rose into your head and imagine that it starts swishing through your sinus channels. As you do this, intend that all the stray thoughts swimming around your head get drawn into the rose. Imagine that other people's thoughts as well as all the stuff you're done processing gets drawn into the rose.
- The rose has infinite space to receive what you're releasing. Notice, as this is going on, if it starts to look different. Do you get any pictures, feelings or messages about what you're letting go of?
- When you're done clearing your head, imagine taking this rose about 1½-2 feet away from your physical body. With your intention, use it to clear the fifth layer of your aura. Intend that the rose is clearing any telepathic congestion that you received from the collective.
- After this is done, toss the rose out to the edge of the horizon, and see it dissolve in a burst of light. As you do, know that the energy you released is getting transmuted into pure creative energy. It will go back where it needs to go.
- Fill in with a gold sun and open your eyes.

CLAIRAUDIENCE AND WORKING WITH SPIRIT GUIDES

Telepathy and clairaudience are both fifth chakra abilities. Clairaudience, or "clear hearing," is your ability to hear both your inner voice and the voice of other spirits or guides. As you read energy clairvoyantly, you may have verbal messages pop into your head to complement what you're seeing. These are clairaudient experiences, and they can also happen spontaneously as you go about your day.

We all have spirit guides, and most of us have many. Some stay with us throughout our lives, and some come just once. Other guides arrive for a period of time when we have something to learn together, and then we move on when the work is done.

Who are your guides? There are ways you can get to know them, and we'll do a meditation to explore this next. Whether you discover their name or cultural background is not so important, because they are currently not in a body. Probably, they've been both male and female, have lived in many places, and had many names. When our guides give us those details, I think it's generally because we shared a past life when they were that person. Or they might show us a certain cultural background because there is something we associate with that culture that we currently need. For example, your guide might present as Buddhist when in fact he's had many other lifetimes. If you are currently learning about mindfulness or other Buddhist philosophies, though, seeing him as Buddhist may help you understand what he's offering you.

I have guides that I recognize by their color and energy, and I've never known them by a name. I may know I connected with them in a certain place geographically, or that they have certain spiritual gifts.

Guides can be teachers, healers, joy guides, animal spirits, nature spirits, angels, ascended masters and more. Whatever you need, you can call a guide to you for that purpose.

Not every spirit is a guide. Death does not make someone enlightened, and some beings are stuck. They may come to you when they're looking for help, or because they like your energy. Some come because they want a drink or because they want to play the piano again. Some spirits are your ancestors, and they may guide and protect you, or they may reinforce old unhealthy patterns from your lineage.

Remember, you are an infinite being, just like they are. Have discernment, and don't feel compelled to listen to every voice or respond to every energy that appears as a spirit around you. Own your power, trust your gut, and if it feels good, go with it. If not, send it to the light. It is easy to do this simply by intending and visualizing it.

You have the precious gift of a body. They don't. You deserve to choose which spirits you do and don't want around. And you have this ability.

Your true guides will sound and feel like wise friends. Whatever you sense or hear from them may only come once, gently. Even if it is firm, there's often a touch of humor. You will probably feel an inner knowing that this is truth—even if you don't like the information and even if it surprises you. No matter the content, wise guidance leaves you feeling clearer and freer. By contrast, an unhelpful spirit may be like that spammer that emails or calls you every day with the same message. These voices sound pushy; they confuse you and just don't feel good. You will know!

Be aware of the questions you ask. A "high-level question" will attract a high-level guide. A question like "How can I make him love me?" or "What are the winning lottery numbers?" will invite in a guide that is less evolved. In the same light, eating healthy and choosing a positive environment will attract more loving guides your way. They live in the realm of energy, so your vibration makes a big difference.

A spirit is not bound by time and space, so there's no limit to how many people they can work with at a time. If Jesus, Buddha, Archangel Michael, or another "popular" guide comes to you, don't discount it. These highly evolved beings don't have a body or worldly matters to attend to, and this freedom and perspective can be very refreshing.

It's important to be intentional when you're working with a guide, and to consciously disconnect when you're done. That way, you choose who is living your life. Even when a highly evolved guide is assisting you, they cannot do your life for you.

As you meet one of your guides in the next meditation, you're not "channeling" the guide, but simply saying hello to them as you would a friend. There are different levels of connection, and we'll discuss this in later chapters.

MEDITATION: MEETING ONE OF YOUR GUIDES

- Sit with your feet on the floor and close your eyes.
- Ground yourself by picturing your tree trunk or waterfall connecting your hips to the center of the earth.
- Soften and let go as you exhale. As you inhale, sit tall and imagine light coming in through the crown of your head.
- Find your point of awareness in the center of your head. As you sit behind your eyes, imagine there's a chair a few feet in front of you.
- Invite one of your helpful spirit guides to take a seat on this chair.
- What do you see? Be open to what your imagination presents. It doesn't have to look like a person, in fact it probably won't. You may just see colored lights or get a flash of something or someone or a symbol. Whatever you get is meaningful to you, so trust it.
- If at any point you don't feel good about this being, you can send them to the light and ask for someone new to appear.
- When you have a being you like in front of you, ask them their name, what they're good at and what they can help you with. Ask them why they want to work with you and how long they've been with you.
- Perhaps they have a message for you now?
- When you're done talking with your spirit guide, thank them and invite them to go back to the light. You can see a gold light appear above their head and that they "fly" through that light back up to source. I like to think of it as sending them off to the astral spa to recharge, knowing you can always call them back at any time.
- Then, see the chair dissolve and notice your breath, body and grounding cord.
- Fill in with a gold sun.

WRITING EXERCISE: GETTING A MESSAGE FROM YOUR GUIDE

1. Take out a pen and paper or use the space below and write a question for your spirit guide. I usually address mine to someone specific, or at least clarify that I'm only inviting in the most beneficial energies of Divine light and love.
2. Once you've written your question, listen for your guide's answer. It's ok if you feel like you're making it up!
3. Write the message back as you're hearing it. Write for as long as you'd like without censoring yourself. Perhaps use your nondominant hand for this part. This can help distinguish your guide's messages from your conscious mind.
4. Pause if you ever sense that the guide talking to you is not of the Light. Send them away and invite in someone new.
5. When you're done, release your guide, ground yourself, and fill in with a gold sun.

WRITING EXERCISE NOTES

CLAIRVOYANCE

Clairvoyance is clear seeing, or the ability to see what's really going on. It's a sixth chakra, or third eye ability, and you can turn it on and off. If images pop into your mind, if you see colors or flashes of light, or even have vivid dreams that provide insight—these can all be clairvoyant experiences. Like the second chakra, the sixth wants to verify that something is real. This is where we say, "Seeing is believing."

Compared to my other psychic senses, I find it easier to be neutral about what I see. When I hear, feel or know things, they seem more "inside me," and so it can get confusing trying to identify where the information is coming from. For example, if your mom sends you a guilt trip and you receive it in your second (feeling) chakra, it's hard not to feel guilty. View that same guilt trip from your third eye (psychic sight), and you might just notice and laugh it off. In part for this reason, I generally teach clairvoyance first with new intuition students.

We "see," clairvoyantly, from the center of our heads. Centering our awareness here while imagining that the thing we're looking at is a few feet in front of us allows us space in relationship to what we're seeing. This way, we can observe something without getting all wrapped up in it. This can be helpful in both recognizing another person's reality as well as seeing our own situations objectively.

MEDITATION: EMPOWERING YOUR CLAIRVOYANCE

- Sit for meditation and ground yourself.
- Bring your attention into your body and breathe.
- Find your awareness in the center of your head. Imagine this space as a bubble of light, a room all your own, or a spot in nature.
- Create a big magnetic soap bubble a few feet out in front of you, outside your energy field/ aura.
- Next, we're going to address the top three obstacles to clairvoyance. One by one, decide that this bubble will pull out of you all the energy that says:
    ◊ *Look at this.* Release any energy you've picked up that says, "This is what you're supposed to see" or "This is what's really going on." Take your time and perhaps observe where it's coming from, which area of your body you're releasing it from, or anything else notable.
    ◊ *Don't look at this.* Let the magnet draw out of you anything that's been blocking you from seeing something that's there. Again, what do you notice about this?
    ◊ *Ignore this.* Let go of any energy that tells you that something real does not exist. Often difficult to recognize, this is where one or more people have obfuscated a matter. Experiencing this can make you feel confused or crazy, and it's very powerful to clear it up. Please know that you don't have to see it to release it. You may feel cloudy or agitated or other sensations as this energy moves out.
- Remember to be amused!
- Once you feel complete, send this bubble off as far as you can imagine and see it explode and dissolve.
- Fill in with a golden sun. If you feel depleted or "off" after these meditations, then more gold suns are in order! Remember to replenish your energy generously.

CLAIRCOGNIZANCE

"I just knew it off the top of my head" is an expression of claircognizance. Also called knowingness, this is your ability to just know something without seeing, hearing or feeling it. This is like a sudden "A-ha, that's what's going on!" It's like climbing to the top of a mountain. After seeing mostly just the details along your path, you get to the top and then see the big picture of where you are.

Knowingness can be revelatory, or it can be ordinary. Besides suddenly understanding big life events or situations, knowingness can include things like:

- Without looking at the clock, you know that it's 2:45 and you need to head out for your 3 pm appointment.
- You know your friend's baby is a girl.
- You know that a certain situation will turn out ok, or that you need to change plans.

Compared to other psychic abilities, I know fewer techniques for turning claircognizance on. Instead, I recommend clearing any related blocks and then creating space for it to arise naturally.

Giving your seniority away to others, experiencing indoctrination or programming, or lacking faith in the Divine are typical reasons this ability gets hijacked. We are going to address these in the next meditation.

To open up to more claircognizance, I recommend meditation or just quiet time. I find that many of my realizations arise in ordinary moments, such as while I'm washing dishes, exercising or driving. Ample sleep and rest can also support inner knowing.

MEDITATION: AWAKENING YOUR INNER KNOWING

- Begin in a seated position where your spine is upright and your feet flat on the floor.
- Center your awareness in your head, ground and breathe.
- Look up to the top of your head and imagine a halo there. This is your crown chakra, the center of your connection to your higher self and the Universe.
- Check that the halo is balanced and fully intact. Adjust it, if not.
- Create a gold, sticky rose and use it to "vacuum" up anything there that's been in the way of your knowing your own answers.
- Notice if there are any bumps or shadow areas, or any colors or pictures that don't seem to belong. Sense if there are people or types of energies influencing this energy center. As these energies disappear, allow your halo to turn a brilliant clear gold.
- When you're complete with this rose, visualize it flying off to the edge of the horizon and see it go "poof" in a burst of light.
- Next, ask yourself a question about your life. Get quiet and allow yourself to receive an "aha" about this. Be receptive to just knowing something, however big or small.
- When you're ready, fill in with a gold sun and come on out of meditation.

MEDIUMSHIP

Mediumship is often seen as the ability to channel a spirit guide. I see it a bit differently. Remembering that you are a spirit in a body, consider that you "channel" your own energy through the vehicle of your physical form. And so first and foremost, I see mediumship as your ability to do this. Here we'll explore your capacity to do that, how conscious you are about it, and how to do it in a way that supports you and the life around you.

Sometimes when people think of psychic abilities, one that comes up is the "out of body experience." People speak of it like it's a rare, magical occurrence. This makes me laugh! Being out of the body is just as common as being in the body. Of course, we need some level of presence to stay alive. But we are multidimensional creatures, and it's amazing how we function with parts of our awareness scattered far and wide. Each time we "space out" and each night when we dream, we've experienced mediumship.

Before exploring your mediumship, it's important to know how to work with your energy "in the body." My teachers in the late 1990s and early 2000s required one year of clairvoyant training first. As the energy has stepped up on the planet, I find most people can learn faster. One real key is learning to ground first, because this energy can be highly expansive.

Mediumship is both very spiritual and very physical. There is a biochemical and genetic component to it. Everyone has the ability and benefits from understanding it, and some of us are more predisposed to it.

I'm going to guide you in learning about your own mediumship—including getting to know this powerful part of yourself, as well as clearing out any toxic influences and outdated patterns. It's not necessary to channel a guide to be a medium, and I won't be teaching channeling in this book. That said, you can talk with spirits without channeling them, which is what I usually recommend. We covered this earlier in Chapter 6, in the exercises following the section on "Clairaudience," and I'll share additional techniques in Chapter 8.

In my experience, the less you do, the more vital your energy will be. I would only want to channel another being if it would raise my vibration to do so. Most people's ancestors, for instance, are not enlightened and do not better the energy of someone who channels them. It's not "bad" to do so and some people have a gift at it, but it's not my focus.

For each of us, our own spiritual energy is meant for our bodies. That's where our bliss is. So, we'll start there. Let's look at some of the ways we enter or leave our bodies:

- At birth
- At death
- When "spacing out" or daydreaming
- In sleeping and waking
- Under the influence of substances, such as drugs, alcohol, caffeine or sugar
- When creating art or music
- When in pain
- During healing work or spiritual practice

The conditions of our transitions affect where we go next. For example, if someone is calm and content at the moment of death, they will tend to go peacefully to the "other side" and next life. Someone who leaves their body—even on a day-to-day basis by spacing out—in numbness or pain winds up with a "cloud" of energy between them and their body. Each subsequent time they check out and try to get back in their body, or even wake up after a night's sleep, they have to get through this thick cloud. The tendency is to disconnect more and more. It's hard to feel clear, present or powerful when you've got this kind of buildup. And it's difficult to pinpoint why you're off-kilter.

The meditation that follows, along with some in the Energy Healing and Manifesting chapter (Chapter 9), will address these issues. We'll practice clearing unconscious mediumship and choosing how we want to enter and leave. From this space of high vibration and with awareness, we can heal ourselves and others.

MEDITATION: RUNNING WHITE

This next meditation begins and ends with grounding. Unlike most of the meditations in this book, the bulk of this practice involves bringing your awareness outside your body. It's important to know how to ground first, so please be sure you have a good handle on the previous meditations before attempting this one.

The benefits of running white energy include gaining perspective on your body and daily life, accessing more of your spiritual power, raising your vibration, and self-healing.

- Begin in a seated position where your spine is upright and your feet flat on the floor.
- Ground yourself, exhale and "land" in your body.
- Run your earth and cosmic energy.
- Center your awareness in the middle of your head.
- Next, take your crown chakra to gold, and then to white.
- As you take it to white, come up to the top of the crown in the back, to the point that would be 12:00 if it were a clock.
- Rest your consciousness at this 12:00 position and notice how you feel.
- Now imagine a bright white loop of energy flowing from your crown chakra down the back of your spine to your root chakra, and then back up the front.
- Let the loop be a continuous circuit as you watch from the top of your crown chakra.
- Cross your ankles or legs, taking your feet off the floor, and release your grounding cord.
- Watch the white loop from the top of your head, and then take your awareness up and out of your body until you are a few feet above your body, looking down.
- Stay here as long as you would like, observing your space. How does it look at white? How do you feel outside your body?

- Looking down at your body, you can send your white light to certain places for healing. I like to bring each of my chakras, glands and aura layers up to white. You can go one by one through different parts of the physical body or the energy body, or just send the white wherever you sense dark, stuck or foreign energy. Perhaps think of a current challenge and ask your white to go anywhere it's needed to heal that issue.
- Use your white light to clear the trans-medium channels, which run down the left and right sides of your spine from the top of the head to below the root. These channels are where your energy—or the energy of another spirit or vibration—comes in. By running your white through these pathways, you claim them for yourself. Pay particular attention to the occipital joints, on either side of the base of the skull. These are spiritual "plug-in" points, where entities attach. If you see dark or muddy energies there, just blast them with light.
- Send some of your white energy above the crown, so you include the first creative ring in your circuit. As you do, you'll clear the space between you and your body, and any "film" that has built up in the threshold.
- The white vibration is very high, quick and simple.
- When you're ready, come back down to the crown chakra and rest your awareness back at the 12:00 position.
- Let the white loop dissolve and be back in your body, breathing.
- Take your crown to all gold.
- Pop down into the center of your head.
- Put your feet flat on the floor, and re-ground yourself.
- Run your earth and cosmic energy. Feel this light shower all around you.
- Bring in a gold sun and open your eyes.
- Return your awareness to your body and surroundings.

Consider what your white vibration is. For me, white equates to love and bliss, and I bring my physical and energetic bodies to that vibration every day. You could choose wholeness, harmony, oneness, infinity, light, peace, or any vibration that resonates for you.

Chapter 7:
READING ANOTHER PERSON

BE PLAYFUL

Your intuition is very close to your imagination. So, when you're receiving information, it often feels like you're "making it up." This is how it *should* feel! You don't make things up out of nowhere. Of all the things you could have conjured up in your mind, why that? If you're triggered, or if you know you're not objective about a particular subject, then definitely take a minute to ground and clear your energy before continuing. In general, setting your space before a reading will assure that you're neutral and sensing accurately.

Even if the thing you're picking up on does not feel helpful, it's still useful to ask why it's showing up and where it's from. Then, communicate the whole of what you see. For example, someone may be throwing negative pictures or judgments at your client. That doesn't mean they're true. You can describe the pictures but also mention that they don't seem to belong to your client. If you get a flash of where they're coming from (for instance: from a female, a male, work, a family member, age five, etc.), say that. This will help the person you're reading decipher and then decide how to handle the situation. It will likely reassure them that they don't have to be so concerned with what's not theirs.

As much as possible, be lighthearted and open as to how information comes in. Getting overly serious may block information from coming. People often discount valuable information because they expect it to come differently. You may think you're going to close your eyes and watch a movie play, but it's rarely like that.

If I say, "Pick a color that represents your best friend," you may get a color but not think much of it. But if I say, "What does that color mean to you? What else do you sense right now about your friend?" and you don't censor yourself, you'll probably receive more information.

Often, you'll pick up on random stuff that you wouldn't attach any meaning to unless you inquired. Turning on your intuition is rarely about finding some secret technique. The more you wonder like a child, the better. The more you get curious and say, "Tell me more about that" rather than thinking, "That's stupid; I give up," the better. Wonder invites answers and magic.

In a class I taught years ago in Pasadena, I'd asked the students to trade readings. For this exercise, one person was to say the name of someone they knew, and the reader was to imagine a rose representing that person and then describe it. As I walked around the room, two young men were struggling. I often need to nudge students at first, but then once they practice a bit, I can't get them to stop talking! These two men were silent, and so I asked the reader what he saw.

"I'm not seeing a rose. I'm just seeing these random pictures," he said.

"That's fine," I replied. "It doesn't have to be a rose. Just say what you see."

It took a minute, but he finally described a very specific car, along with a Hawaiian shirt. The other guy's jaw dropped open.

"I asked you about my dad," he said. "That's the car he drives, and he's going to Hawaii tomorrow."

Ever since witnessing this, I do my best to share any "random" pictures I get, because you never know how much it will mean to someone. I frequently tell a client, "I don't know why, but I'm seeing X." I don't understand it, but she'll know exactly what it means. It's the same for your own life. If you meditate and get a flash of something, or if you're going through your day and have a thought pop in "out of the blue," get curious about it.

When I receive seemingly bizarre or incomplete information, I love to ask, "Tell me more about this." It's amazing how simply asking for more will bring more. That moment when it would be so easy to shut down and say, "I don't know" is the very moment to get inquisitive. Even if the next piece of information is just a word, a color, a person's face or an age—it will all come together to form a story, if you stay patient and have fun with the process.

Keeping your sense of humor up not only allows you to see more; it also facilitates healing. Pain lives in our blind spots, and awakening intuition brings it up to be cleared. Fortunately, it's hard to be in pain when you're laughing.

ETHICS AND INTEGRITY

Years ago, I frequently offered readings and talks at holistic expos. On one occasion, another psychic reader approached me without invitation. She started telling me about a man I would meet in New Orleans, a place she claimed I was strongly connected to. Her reading felt "off" to me and 15 years later, I have neither felt drawn to New Orleans nor have I met that man.

Fortunately, I am not that gullible. I never took that in. Often, people go to spiritual healers and teachers when they are feeling vulnerable, and they can be easily programmed. This makes ethics very important.

After working with one client on improving his health for some time, he told me a previous reader had predicted he would get cancer. Ten or more years later, he has not had cancer and he's followed a holistic lifestyle. I don't know if he would or wouldn't have gotten sick otherwise, but I cannot support simply making a negative prediction for someone. In my opinion, being ethical is being honest while also empowering people.

To check your ethics, consider how you say things as well as your inner motivations. Are you most interested in being right, being impressive, or being helpful? As you receive information and consider what to share, I recommend asking internally something like "Does this give to life?" or "Does this serve love?" If those answers are "no," then I would refrain from speaking certain things, even if you think they are accurate.

Looking for "the question behind the question" is wonderful if you do it to be more helpful, and you sense the readiness for a deeper conversation. However, disregarding someone's question or request because you're drawn to talk about something else is not ethical. If you feel so inspired, ask yourself if that story you're about to tell will actually benefit them. It's possible that it relates to their intention, or that their soul is showing you something they're reluctant to ask directly. If you sense it may serve them, you can always give them a quick snapshot and ask them if they'd like to know more. Honor their choice.

You may receive sensitive information that you're not sure about relaying to the person you're reading. When this happens for me, I'll ask internally, "Should I say this? How?" Generally, I'll hear the answer. Sometimes I'll feel sensations in my body, or I'll see a bright light or a brick wall. You will get the clues you need, if you ask and observe what comes to you.

Whether you do professional readings or not, these guidelines apply. Friends, family members and lovers also influence each other and may be extra sensitive at vulnerable times. In addition, it's harder to keep clean boundaries when you know someone well. You may find it impossible to be objective. They may resist you and not want insight. Don't push if they indicate this.

If you do give or receive readings or healings with people you know, loving and respectful intentions as well as permission are even more important here. I find it works best to set aside a time separate from your friendship or family time. I also recommend being specific about who is giving or receiving at any given time, and clearly preparing and disconnecting before and after each reading. For example, take 15 minutes for each person with a few minutes in-between for each of you to switch roles. This should minimize projection or unnecessary emotional involvement, and it gives each of you more of what you're needing.

To sum up, here are a few tips for using your intuition with integrity:

- Only read when asked or given permission. If the person in question is not physically present, ask psychically if it's ok to read them.
- If you sense something sensitive while reading, pause and ask internally how / if to share it.
- Respect a "no" if you get one or even if there is no answer.
- Set clear boundaries as noted above, such as designating a time separate from your personal relating, when exchanging readings with people you know.

I believe my clients show me what I see. I'm not a peeping Tom! The easiest people to read are those who are curious and on a path of personal development. The hardest people to read are those who aren't really open, who are simply testing me.

    Don't get discouraged if you can't see something. The person in question may not wish to show you that, or it might be best not to know right now. For instance, sometimes we have to "walk through" certain experiences in order to learn and grow, before our future can be revealed. If you could see where you're going ahead of time, you might not become the person you need to be to get there. Frequently, you'll be shown the next step for yourself or your client, but not the outcome. Not being able to see something is rarely due to your lack of skill, and it's more likely that you're simply not being shown. No answer is still an answer! Look for the opening and start there, offering whatever seems most clear and helpful now.

READING WITH PURPOSE

Reading others is also for you. I'm not suggesting that you project your stuff onto people, but to keep in mind that you have a say over everything you experience. You can decide how you are going to show up and invite each reading to teach you something valuable. After all, you wouldn't want to read people if it didn't give you anything! That's ok.

If you're struggling with confidence, with finding your voice, or with clearly interpreting the information you receive—decide to overcome that challenge when you give your next reading. When you need help understanding your patterns with relationships, work or money—ask the Universe to send you people who will show you what you need to know. You may have a special interest in supporting certain types of clients, or people going through specific situations. I was a psychic teenager with no mentor, so I personally love it when sensitive young people find me. Having spent a few years in my 20s as a singer/songwriter, I've attracted lots of musicians. This is fun for me, and I "get" their world. In addition, I have a passion for masculine-feminine dynamics, conscious relationships, and holistic health. You have unique gifts and life experience that many people could benefit from! Call them to you.

While neutrality is important, an inherent part of being alive is our interconnectedness. The first time I gave a clairvoyant reading in class, I left crying. This was not because I was traumatized. I felt confused in a sense, wondering if I was really "reading" because I identified so deeply with the person in front of me. While his profile and circumstances were different than mine, I profoundly sensed how we humans are more alike than different. This shocked me into a deeper compassion that has grown since that day. As Ram Dass said, "We are all walking each other home."

MEDITATION: SETTING AN INTENTION FOR YOUR READINGS

Before you read another person, I recommend doing this next exercise. Besides helping you learn, grow and serve at a greater level, this also creates some psychic protection for you as you open to others' energy.

Some clients show up with big problems and tons of stress. No matter what, it's not your problem. You won't help them more by assuming it is. Without your own intention for the reading, it can be tempting to try to heal or fix the person in front of you. You could get stuck in effort, thinking that you have to perform for them, and then end up seeing nothing. If you're letting their expectations control you, you won't be able to tell them anything new and you'll both walk away feeling worse. So, at least, decide that you're going to learn and grow and enjoy the experience. You'll both win that way.

Once you get the hang of setting your reading intentions, I think you'll find this to be quick, fluid and well worth it! You can do this next exercise on your own, as a way to call in the clients and readings you want, or in the presence of someone you're about to read. Just allow a few minutes of quiet for it.

- Sit in meditation, breathe and ground.
- Run your cosmic and earth energy.
- Find the center of your head. Create plenty of space there for you.
- Now, imagine a bubble a few feet out in front of you.
- Consider what you'd like to learn, how you'd like to feel, and what you'd like to offer when you give intuitive readings. Do you want answers about your job or love life? Or, to understand how your father's energy affected you? Would you like to heal sadness? Do you want to feel more confident or more amused in your readings? Would you prefer receptive, easy-to-read clients? Or those who quiz you on their deceased grandmother's favorite foods? How about working with artists, athletes, mothers or entrepreneurs? What inspires you?
- See those pictures in the bubble. If visual imagery doesn't come so

easily, you might simply sense a color, feel the feelings, or focus on your positive thoughts.
- Once you've imagined it, send the bubble out to the Universe to dissolve into a burst of light. You're now ready to begin reading.

CHOOSING YOUR READING COLOR

Now, pick someone to read! It's fine to meet in person, or over the phone or video conference. Because hearing someone's voice will help you tap in and facilitates more fruitful dialogue, I do not recommend doing these exercises over email or written messages alone.

Once you have another person in front of you, I suggest setting a reading color. To do this, you'll take your crown chakra to a certain color, which you'll determine case-by-case for each reading. I recommend this for two reasons. First, this helps you get "on the same page" as the person you are reading, so that you understand them better. Second, it ensures that you maintain a distinction between your energy and theirs. This will make the experience clearer for both of you. Here's how to choose your reading color:

- Have your readee sit a few feet away from you (long distance via Internet or phone is also fine), with their feet on the floor and eyes open. In most cases, in person, this makes them easier to see because they remain more present.
- As you sit in meditation with your eyes closed, ask them to say their full name aloud three times.
- Notice the first color that comes to mind as they say their name. This is the primary color they are resonating with, right now.
- Pick a color that's similar yet easy to distinguish from their color. For example, if you saw green for your client, you could choose blue or yellow for yourself. Even a subtle shift—such as from forest green to lime green— can also work.
- This second color is your reading color. Set your crown chakra to this color by imagining a halo of this color at the top of your head.
- Open your eyes and let your readee know you are ready to begin! Then, move immediately to the next section, where I walk you through giving a simple clairvoyant reading.

PRACTICE: GIVING A ROSE READING

- After you've completed the previous two exercises to set your intention and your reading color, you're ready to start reading.
- Ask the person you're reading to sit with their feet on the floor, and eyes open.
- Ask your readee to say their name out loud three times, again.
- With your eyes closed as you hear their name, imagine a rose out in front of you that represents their energy in present time.
- Just like you did for yourself earlier, study the qualities of this rose. What state of bloom is it in? What color? Does it have a stem? Thorns? Where is it growing, or is it?
- Describe what you see, and then interpret it. If this rose were a person, what do you know about this person by looking at the rose? Communicate this.
- When you're done, explode the rose.
- If you and your readee wish, you could repeat this exercise with different roses representing different areas of their life. They might like you to take a look at their love life, soul's purpose, health, money, someone they know, a project or opportunity, or other topics. Have them say a few words about each area before you read it.
- Destroy each rose before proceeding to the next rose.
- When you're done, fill in with a gold sun.
- Open your eyes, and chat with your readee about what just happened!

MEDITATION: CLEARING AND REPLENISHING AFTER YOU READ OTHERS

Just as I recommend setting your space before giving a reading, it's also important to clear your field after you complete a reading and before you go on with your day. Here is an exercise to walk you through this:

- Just after completing a reading, imagine a big magnetic soap bubble a few feet out in front of you.
- Exhale, and imagine anything you took on during the reading that wasn't yours goes into the soap bubble. Energy from your readee, from people or beings connected to them, or from anyone else in the environment can go now. Let the bubble take it so you don't take it with you.
- In addition, allow this bubble to absorb anything within you that may have been triggered by the reading—whatever you're ready to release. This could be feelings of not being good enough, competition or fear of speaking up. You may feel a charge because of something you saw which mimics something in your own life. If you have similar challenges, beliefs or emotions that aren't serving you—go ahead and use this time to clear these things from your field. Let them go into the bubble.
- Look and see what you're releasing. Ask for guidance. Remember: you don't need to know what you're letting go of. It will clear regardless. Have faith that you'll see the pictures and have the awareness that benefits you, and yet be thankful you don't have to see it all!
- Once you feel complete with this release process, send the bubble to the edge of the horizon, and watch it pop into a burst of light.
- Be behind your eyes and check back in with your body and energy flowing. Allow your crown chakra to go back to whatever color you like. Gold works well, or any color in the rainbow.
- Finally, create a big gold sun above your head. Besides the usual people and places, future and past, call your energy back from the

reading. Let the sun hold all the Divine light that is meant for you, and then drink it in like liquid gold nectar. Let it simmer throughout and around you as you open your eyes.

INTERPRETING ENERGY AND COMMUNICATING WHAT YOU SEE

As I teach people to read energy, I am often asked about interpretation and communication. And so, at this point I thought it may help to have a quick reference of tips given throughout the book thus far:

- With any energy you're curious about in your life, visualize a gauge and ask what percentage is or isn't yours. Or when someone else tells you about their problem or desire, you can use this same gauge to discover what percentage belongs to them. In both cases, inquire as to how much is happening in present time. These answers offer valuable understanding and distinctions.
- Look at whether the colors you see are clear or muddy. Both dark and light colors belong to the person you're reading if they are clear and luminous. Murky-looking energy is generally either stuck or belonging to someone else.
- If you see something sensitive, before speaking to your readee, ask your guides or higher self, "Am I meant to say this? If so, how?" Listen and follow whatever guidance resonates with you.
- Don't expect yourself to see everything or solve every problem. Be willing to say, "I'm not being shown that," "I see a blank screen," or "The person you're asking about doesn't want to talk now… or doesn't want a healing." There are times when these answers are the truth, and the truth is helpful even if it's not what someone thinks they want. Be gentle, but don't force. Trying to find something that's not there doesn't serve anyone.
- Practice! The more you practice and get feedback, the more you'll trust your accuracy in interpreting energy.
- If a symbol or picture does not make sense to you, perhaps describe it literally and ask, "What does this mean to you?" Don't feel like you have to understand everything. It may make sense to you or your client now or later. Trust what comes to the surface now.

THE ART OF MATCHING ENERGY WITHOUT MERGING

While you've learned in this book to stay in your space and clear other people's energy out, there are times you may want to "match" another person's energy. This is different from merging because you're not confusing your energy with theirs, nor does it take anything from either of you.

Setting your reading color is one way to (almost) match someone's energy. In this case, you do it so you can see more psychically, and to better support the other person. It's done consciously, and you go back to being yourself after the reading.

Let's say a friend tells you about something exciting in her life and you feel a rush of enthusiasm. "Maybe this could happen to me too!" you think. You just matched her energy. In some cases, it's less specific. For instance, you feel more confidence or inner peace after being with someone who feels those things. You may not want the exact life they're having, but you can still enjoy the energy and use it as you wish.

Besides matching energy spontaneously, you can also do it proactively. Let's say you desire a happy love life or a certain level of wealth. Observe whenever you see this in the world around you. Go to those neighborhoods. Watch those movies and ask those people questions like "What's your secret?" Then, emulate what they do, think and feel. Literally imagine yourself fluttery in love, or as if money is no problem—if these are the experiences you're desiring.

Matching other people is not always helpful; it can also cause problems. Common examples of this are indoctrination or cultural programming. If everyone around you has a certain set of assumptions, it's easy to take these beliefs on as your own. Even in your household or social group, things "rub off on you." For instance, I've heard success coaches say that your income can be predicted by the top five people you hang out with. And so, spending lots of time with people who are struggling (in any area) is not likely to support you.

All of the above are examples of "matching" energy, and they differ from "merging" energy. So far in this book, we've discussed "merging," which encompasses both what you absorb from others as well as what they absorb from you. For instance, taking on a particular person's pain or receiving their judgments are forms of merging energy. Giving your power away and over-focusing on other people are also ways to merge.

By contrast, matching is less personal, less directed. It's more about you or the other person shifting vibration rather than exchanging energy. It's based in the assumption that we are each already infinite, and that we don't need to go outside ourselves to get anything. It's just like tuning our radio dial to the channel we'd like to listen to.

In either case, good boundaries and awareness are essential. There are times you'll want to feel what others are feeling to a degree. There are ways to do that while also maintaining your neutrality. Hopefully, as you practice setting your reading color at a hue slightly different from the person you're reading, you'll get a feeling for when you're matching energy in everyday life.

Just as you can match another person's or group's energy, other people can match yours. Do not underestimate the power of your simple presence, or of the frequency you put out. To become more conscious of this, play with broadcasting positive energy for others to match. Notice how you affect those around you, and perhaps jot these experiences down in your Intuition Journal.

We can also match the energy of a place. For instance, have you ever gone into a home or business that had great "vibes?" You probably felt good just being there. Years ago, my family moved to Colorado from a large condominium complex in LA. With a few comparable rentals open in the building, the woman who took over our rental expressed that our condo felt very different and that she had to have it! She said she could feel all the meditation and spiritual practice that had happened there.

All the energy cultivation you do, all that you have learned and have healed within yourself is available for anyone around you to match. When many people do this in one place, it's palpable. However, even one person can make a difference. If you are neutral in an area where someone else is stuck, you help them get free without saying a word! We'll discuss this more in the section on healing coming up.

Chapter 8:
SPECIAL READING TOPICS

HOW TO PRACTICE THESE READINGS

In this chapter, we'll get into the specifics of how to do readings for different situations. While the instructions describe how to do each exercise for yourself, each of these readings can be done with another person. I recommend exploring each one first on your own, so you get a feeling for it. This will also allow you to have your own healing and understanding, and it will give you more to offer others.

Before reading another person, be sure to set your space and intentions, and then clean out and replenish afterwards. Communicate as you go, using the tips given in the previous chapter on reading others.

RELATIONSHIP READINGS

The most frequent questions I get from clients are about relationships. Besides romantic connections, you can use your intuition to better understand any type of relationship. You might be curious about the dynamics between family members, co-workers, roommates, friends or any other important people in your life.

For any relationship to be successful, each individual needs to do their part. If someone does not love themselves, is unavailable, or has a lot of subconscious roadblocks, this will limit any relationship they have with anyone. That said, each relationship has particular patterns and agreements at play. When I read the connection between two people, I take a peek at the relationship space itself, as well as how each person relates with it.

While each situation is unique, here are some common things to look for:

- Does each person have enough energetic space in this relationship? Are they allowed to be and express themselves?
- Is there foreign energy from others affecting the relationship space?
- What is the purpose of this relationship? Does each person's individual purpose align with this?
- Are the relationship agreements healthy and relevant, or do they need to be updated?
- What cycle is this relationship in? Are there new beginnings, is there growth potential, or is it coming to completion?
- Are old wounds affecting the relationship space? Can these relationship triggers become fuel for personal growth?
- How much energy is each person is putting into the relationship? It is in balance?

Perhaps this list has got you thinking about one or more of your relationships. The following exercise will guide you to do a reading so you can gain insight.

PRACTICE: READING A RELATIONSHIP

- Sit in meditation, ground yourself and run your earth and cosmic energy.
- Find the center of your head and aura bubble.
- Think of a person you're having a challenge with, or a relationship you'd like to improve or understand more clearly.
- In your mind's eye, imagine three roses out in front of you. The one on the left represents you, the one on the right is the other person, and the one in the middle represents the relationship.
- Observe the colors, sizes, state of bloom, and other qualities of each rose. Note the length of their stems and any thorns, leaves or other features in the environment.
- If you were to make up a story about each person and their relationship based on what you see in these roses, what would you say?
- Is there any energy that is not serving each person or the relationship itself? You might sense this as dark or cloudy areas, or perhaps you see specific pictures or symbols.
- How much energy is each person putting into this relationship? Is it in balance? If you'd like, imagine a pie chart and see how much Person A is putting in and how much Person B is putting in. Then, dissolve the chart.
- Visualize a gold sun above each rose, representing the purpose of each person and the relationship. Notice whether or not each rose is lined up with the sun above it. This will allow you to see if the relationship is fulfilling its purpose, as well as whether each individual is "on purpose" within it.
- Explore anything else you would like to about this connection, then dissolve each rose and the pictures you're seeing.
- Fill yourself in with a gold sun, and then come out of meditation.

PAST LIVES + KARMA

What is karma? Simply, it's the law of cause and effect. For every action, there is a reaction. All of our actions—even thoughts—create consequences in this life or another. Understanding this gives a heightened importance to everything we do. It's the Universe's way of keeping balance and it's part of how our souls evolve. Right now, you are surely experiencing the results of your actions from past lives as well as this one.

While it's often viewed as heavy or punishing, my teacher used to say, "Karma is God giving us another chance." I love this! It reminds us that we are always seeking love and wholeness, and it gives us a nudge to avoid repeating negative patterns.

I do believe things are changing on Earth—from a more karmically determined way of living to one that is more evolution-based. Our actions still have consequences, yet it feels like we have more choices as the collective light and awareness has grown. We have left the Age of Pisces, which was more codependent and more about completion. Now, in the Age of Aquarius, we are creating new ways of living, relating and accessing spirituality. Our emerging world is a world of mutual gifting, creativity and community, rather than obligation and reaction.

We can have karma with a person, group, place or situation. Here are some examples:

- Two people who were in love yet unable to be together in a past life may feel instant "chemistry" and intense magnetism.
- Places where you've been in past lives bring up emotions, a sense of familiarity, or a feeling like you "have to" go there.
- You become a healer because you harmed others in the past.
- After moving to a new community or starting a new class or job, you feel like you've been with these people before, and that you all have a shared purpose together.
- You inherit money or land because you gave in a past life.
- That person you feel you need to take care of all the time used to be your child.

- In many past lives you were a slave or in service jobs, and so have trouble feeling free, worthy or successful in this lifetime.
- As a past king, queen or leader, you abused your power and so are called to humility or integrity this go-round.

Past lives are entertaining, but that's not enough reason for me to look at them. Typically, I see them when someone is dealing with a powerful relationship or a repeating pattern. If conditions in this life don't seem to explain a certain situation, then understanding the relevant past lives will likely shed light.

Occasionally, clients ask me about past lives without a specific reason. In these cases, I ask to see whatever would benefit them now. Past life readings can offer a spiritual recognition that looking at this life alone does not. Certain souls have always been artistic or spiritual, natural teachers or leaders or warriors, or talented with gardening or building or healing. Some have been learning mindfulness or playfulness or humility or confidence for eons. I've even met folks with roots in other galaxies. In the next meditation, you'll learn to see past lives. Have fun!

As you tap into a past life, the whole storyline is not important. Just decide that you will see what you or your readee need to know. And remember, we have all been both male and female and lived in many cultures. What you see is one very small slice of a soul's story. It's showing up as a gift to activate more evolution from here on out.

MEDITATION: SEEING A PAST LIFE

- Sit with your feet flat on the floor and ground yourself.
- Run your earth and cosmic energy.
- Find your sanctuary space in the center in your head and balance your aura bubble.
- Think about a person, place or situation you would like to see your past life with.
- Envision a big movie screen out in front of you. For now, it is blank.
- Imagine you have a jar of marbles next to you and, as you ask your question about a past life, pick one marble that "lights up." Throw that marble onto your screen.
- Watch as the screen starts to show you the images that represent your previous life. You may also feel, hear, know or sense things. Ask what any symbols, colors or messages represent.
- Ask why you are seeing this. What is the message that will most help you at this time, in this life?
- When you feel complete for now, dissolve the image and your screen.
- Fill in with a gold sun, retrieving your energy from that past life and integrating all the wisdom gained.

WHAT ARE THE AKASHIC RECORDS?

Your records from all your lifetimes as well as your probable future are stored in the Akashic Hall of Records. As psychic students, we took spiritual "field trips" to this spot within the etheric planes. It was fun to read the records and help keep them straight.

Meanwhile, you have a personal Akashic record keeper—a guide who stays with you from lifetime to lifetime. S/he keeps your files updated so that you don't have to keep processing the same stuff over and over. In my view, your record keeper moves information from your energy field into what looks like a column outside your space. It's like taking files off your desktop and moving them onto your external hard drive. This gives you space to think straight and move forward, and it frees you from mental and emotional loops. If you ever need the information in storage, you can still retrieve it. But think about this. I bet if you ever go through old paperwork, you realize how little you've needed it in years! It's similar with your Akashic records.

Periodically, you can ask your record keeper to update your files, just like you spring clean your closets or do your weekly laundry. I especially recommend this after a major transition or time of intense processing. This way, you stay current with your life and become freer in your consciousness. You'll move through changes more quickly and with more grace.

When you feel your energy entangled with another's and cannot seem to shift it on your own, call both your Akashic record keeper and theirs. Ask them to bring each person's energy back to their own bodies. Our record keepers know us and what belongs to us better than any guide, and they come with neutrality when we are too close to a situation to fully see or change it.

MEDITATION: MEETING YOUR AKASHIC RECORD KEEPER AND UPDATING YOUR RECORDS

- Ground, center yourself, and run your energy.
- A few feet out in front of you, create a stage or a screen. Let it be blank or empty for now.
- Next, invite your Akashic record keeper to appear on the stage or screen. What do you notice?
- Get to know your guide. Ask them questions, such as "When were my records last updated?" or "Where is my energy right now, besides in my body?"
- Ask your guide to update your records. You can request this in a general sense, or for any specific goals you have. For example, you might say, "Please refresh my information about relationships, work or health," after experiencing changes in one of those areas. Ask for help renewing your self-concept or beliefs about the world around you. Consider an update after a family member is born or dies, after a move, or as you engage in spiritual practice, therapy or coaching. When you're in school or have just learned a new skill, you will also want to get your files in order.
- What do you notice as your guide completes the update? Take as long as you'd like here, and then thank your guide once finished.
- Fill in with a gold sun and replenish!

CONNECTING WITH SOULS WHO HAVE PASSED

When my grandfather died, I sat down in meditation to say hello. Closing my eyes, I had barely put my attention on him when I heard his voice the way he always answered the phone. "Longs," he proclaimed with enthusiasm. It was as if he didn't know he had died.

If you have a loved one who has passed, you may relate to this ease of connection, as if they are right there. If you aren't sure you're sensing them clearly and feel like you're imagining things, it's likely you're not. Getting out of your own way helps! There is such a thin veil between worlds, so let it be easy. If you're still having trouble noticing someone's presence, they may not be fully available for various reasons.

It's a misunderstanding to think that all spirits are enlightened. It's a long haul—this journey of the soul—and changing form does not instantly erase our challenges. Your ancestors and people you knew personally are likely not as evolved as spirit guides, such as angels or ascended masters. While death means one no longer needs to go to work or deal with the body's grumblings, the afterlife can be a time of intense processing and integration. I see this for all souls to some degree. The more one is aware in one's life, the greater amount of light they experience after death. Therefore, souls that died in peace tend to feel both more accessible and more helpful.

When someone asks me about a loved one that died in suicide, in a car crash, or other "shock" death, the departed one often looks stuck. This is because the condition of consciousness at the moment of transition colors the experience going forward. Often, these beings need a lot of healing before they go "to the light." They can be in a limbo state for quite some time, and it can be very painful. When I am asked about such cases, I tend to do more healing than reading—helping these souls get free. Most times they don't have much to say.

Just like with any reading, no answer is still an answer. Seeing that someone is stuck—or that they just need time to orient before they can talk with you—is still information. While my client may ache to have a conversation or feel her loved one's warmth, at least knowing where they're at can provide some solace and understanding.

It's possible your ancestors are around you as spirit guides, and they generally do care about you very much! However, their advice and influence will be filtered through their personalities. I always recommend asking if this feels relevant and uplifting to you. If not, it's ok to disregard their advice and just release them to the light.

As a reminder, you can stay fully present and don't need to "channel" to talk to a spirit. The next meditation will guide you through connecting with someone who has passed away.

MEDITATION: COMMUNICATING WITH SPIRITS

- Find a comfortable meditation spot, breathe and connect to yourself.
- See your tree trunk or other grounding cord dropping down from your hips to the core of the earth, and then let go of what you don't need.
- Rub your feet on the floor until you feel a little tingle, and then allow the earth energy to flow up through your legs and back down to your grounding.
- Sit tall and draw light in through your crown, down your spine, and up the front, showering it out the top of your head at the end.
- Be behind your eyes in your own personal sanctuary.
- Consider someone you know who has passed away.
- "Imagine" where they are. Perhaps you see a screen out in front of you on which they appear. Say hello and notice if you get a reply back.
- How do they look? What do you sense about their state of being? What are they saying to you? Give yourself a few minutes to observe and dialogue, if they are available.
- Ask them any specific questions or share anything you're drawn to share.
- When you're ready, thank them and release them, and dissolve your screen.
- Create a big golden sun above your body. Put a magnet in it, and then allow this magnet to call all of your energy back from people and places, future and past. Let it fill with all that's yours by Divine right, and then see that it floods your entire body and energy body with light.

BABY BEINGS

Baby beings tend to hang out around the parents they're hoping to have. They've been known to break condoms and are the best matchmakers! On occasions such as miscarriage, they come in briefly, and then go. From a higher perspective, these experiences are a healing opportunity for the would-be parents. Like all spirits, baby beings know no time and space, yet are rarely enlightened. They have missions—and therefore pick the parents and life circumstances that will help them achieve what they're here for.

Just because a baby spirit is around does not mean that someone should or will have that baby. A parent-child relationship is based on the free will of both parties. Often, agreements are made before we incarnate, and so psychic readings can reveal strong probabilities. We can also pick up information about a baby spirit's history, personality, life goals and contracts with Mom, Dad or others.

You can do a reading and ask about baby beings, or you may spontaneously sense one around you or a friend. My daughter first revealed herself to me over 15 years before I had her, when I was a budding singer/songwriter. In meditation, she showed me that she loved music and wanted to learn certain relationship lessons. In the midst of learning those lessons myself, I said, "How about I heal this first and *then* bring you in?" I was young and had no steady partner, home or career at the time. At the suggestion of a friend (who, one day, put his hands around my belly and told me about her spirit without my even mentioning it!), I did a ceremony for her, and she left for quite some time.

By the time my daughter's soul returned, I had a partner who was solid and reliable. However, he did not want a child. I felt her so strongly, and I knew I had to have her, so the man and I parted ways. A year and a half later, I found myself putting everything in storage and traveling for months following my inner guidance. I ended up meeting my daughter's father, and we started dating, even though neither of us felt the other was "our type." Turns out he was getting messages from her too. We got pregnant on the first try, and it's clear that she was playing Cupid, setting the whole thing up.

When my daughter was still in the womb, her dad had a spontaneous picture of her snowboarding. At that time, we had no idea we'd be moving from LA to Colorado.

I felt her love of music and water back then. She got happy when I waded in a river, soaked in a hot tub, or even took a shower. I'd feel her dancing in my belly and she'd say, "I really like this one," when a fun song came on. Now at eight years old, she is learning several instruments and has written more than a dozen songs. She'll wander off and I'll find her singing. "My angels were giving me a new song, Mama," she'll say. She has a notebook where she's starting to write them down.

Not everyone has such clear images of their babies to come. I've worked with many a mother-to-be who yearns to know if there's a child out there for her. I've worked with pregnant ladies who wonder about the soul coming in, what they need, and what their agreements are. You can learn to do readings to determine if you or someone else has baby spirits around. Let's try it.

PRACTICE: SEEING BABY BEINGS

- Find a cozy meditation spot, breathe and bring your awareness into your body.
- Check your grounding cord, and update it as needed.
- Run your earth and cosmic energy.
- Next, you are going to look at any agreements you have with baby beings. If you already have children, this is one way to learn more about your agreements with them. If not, you may see potential babies to come, or you may see souls you have not wished to bring in. That's ok. It's also possible you have no contracts at all. Let's explore.
- From the center of your head, imagine a rose a few feet out in front of you. This rose represents yourself.
- Pay special attention to the stem. Each leaf on the stem indicates an agreement you have with a baby being. How many do you see?
- If you don't see any baby contracts, perhaps pause here and find someone else who would like a reading on this topic. Or consider asking about other agreements you have, such as with your parents.
- As you examine the leaves, notice if some are bigger or smaller. Are any more or less robust? This could mean that certain agreements are stronger, or perhaps some souls have louder personalities. I was taught that leaves closer to the rose are closer to incarnating, and that leaves farther down were more distant or less likely.
- Play with what you see and what it means to you. Ask about anything you'd like, such as gender, timing, their life goals and why they chose you.
- When you're ready, watch from behind your eyes as you dissolve the rose, leaves and stem.
- Create a giant golden sun and replenish your energy from head to toe. Open your eyes.

PSYCHIC KIDS

As a child, did you hear any of these types of messages?

"Stop crying. There's no monster under the bed."

"No, honey, I'm not angry… I'm fine."

"That's just your imaginary friend."

Unfortunately, most of us experienced this kind of invalidation growing up. Because the adults around us didn't see what we saw, they told us it didn't exist. While there are exceptions, our caregivers usually meant well. It's just that their generation had much less permission to be psychic than we do! However, we still need to clear these old imprints if we are to fully rekindle our spiritual capacities.

Children live largely in the spiritual world. If you spend time with kids or have your own, you can also take notes from how they "wonder" about things. The more we can encourage them, the less they will have to relearn later. Because they are so open, their intuition springs forth naturally if not stopped.

Incarnating is not instant; it is a process. In the womb, the child's soul is in and out of the forming body. Babies sleep a lot because their souls are gently touching down into the body. The babies slowly increase their waking hours as the souls get used to earthly life. Meanwhile, their crown chakra stays open during the first year or two of life, as evidenced by their soft spot on the top of the head. This keeps them close to God and it's why we can feel such bliss around babies!

In my years working with children and now as a mother, I have seen firsthand how kids light up when someone sees at their level! By contrast, I remember when a father picked up his elementary-aged daughter from a creativity class I had taught. When the girl proudly showed him her drawing of a spirit she saw, he turned to me and said, "Are they all this weird?" I was disheartened, yet glad I could be a support for her.

Kids' psychic abilities are not always this dramatic. For example, in Aikido we practice feeling when our training partner is open, sensing when to assert ourselves versus when to turn and let them pass. This is a basic life skill that is based in intuition.

Children tend to feel and express the energy they pick up from parents, siblings and the world around them. When my daughter was just two days old, she started crying when her dad and I argued about the laundry. I really took note. Of course, we humans will argue and be imperfect. I knew though that I wanted her to have the tools to stay centered, so she didn't take on our stuff—or anyone else's. Since then, I have taught her to do this in age-appropriate ways, and she is very much her own person now. I have also validated her experiences of sensing energy, and we often talk with her departed grandmothers over dinner!

Next, I'll go over some simple practices that you can share with any children in your life. Most of these will be familiar, as they are variations on the adult meditations you've already learned. In general, kids are better at imagining than we adults, and they shift energy faster than we do. So keep it simple, have fun, and be open to learning from the children around you.

ENERGY AWARENESS EXERCISES FOR KIDS

Grounding

Children who are hyperactive or overly emotional may simply need a good meal or a nap! That said, I also like to teach them to ground by imagining a connection from their hips to the center of the earth. Given a choice, I've had kids ground using ice cream cones or rockets as well as tree trunks and light beams. Remember—the more playful we can be, the more intuition works. So I encourage it!

I have definitely seen kids calm down after grounding. To make it better, have them do it outside or add some good exhales. They don't have to sit. Perhaps they stand and bend their knees as they feel the grounding cord dropping down from their tailbones.

Bye-Bye Bubble

At the end of the day, or after an emotional upset or minor bump or fall, young kids can use a "bye-bye bubble" to let go of whatever didn't feel good. Literally, get a jar of soap bubbles with a wand if you want to get playful. Otherwise, just have them imagine it. You can tell a child, "Make a bubble. Now put whatever you didn't like today in the bubble."

They might name things such as: boo-boos, loud noises, tummy aches, spilled ice cream cones, mean kids, not getting to do their favorite thing, etc. You can suggest things too. I recommend letting them know they can clear their parents' and siblings' energy, for example that Mom's sadness is not their responsibility. If you are the parent doing this meditation with them, they will definitely know you love them. And remember, you are still connected by the cord at your root chakra. As you give them ideas about what to put in the bye-bye bubble, add in any other people or things that you suspect might be affecting them. Keep it light, and trust in their higher selves.

Always do the following "sunshine" meditation after the Bye-Bye Bubble. It can be quick, but it's important that they replenish their energy.

Sunshine

Here's how I guide a child in the gold sun meditation:

"Make a sunshine above your head. Now, make the sunshine full of (CHILD'S NAME)'s energy. Put a magnet in it and call yourself back from school, the park, Grandma's house (name any places they've been.) If you've been thinking about anybody or anything, bring your energy back from there into the sun. Let all your golden light fill up the sun. Now, take a deep breath and let the sunshine pour into your body. Fill your body up with (CHILD'S NAME)'s light.

Bedtime Meditation: Intentions

One way to minimize nightmares and sleep interruptions is to help kids feel more "in charge" of their sleep experience. I let my daughter know that when her body rests, her spirit gets to play.

"What would you like to do tonight?" you can ask your child. Then, bedtime becomes more fun. Here are some dream time suggestions if you need them: going to the beach or other nature spot, seeing friends or family, or practicing an activity they love—such as music or basketball. I swear my daughter plays piano in her dreams, because somehow she keeps getting better without practicing!

Bedtime Meditation: Colors

As they're getting ready for bed, ask your child to pick a relaxing color for their bedroom. Imagine together that you fill the room with that colored light. In addition, ask them what color feels good around their body as they go to sleep. Have them picture a bubble of that color around them.

Of course, you can use this practice when they're awake as well. For instance, "What color bubble do you want for your soccer game?" or "What color makes you feel strong or happy or more focused?" Show them they can use this to regulate their emotions, to do better at school, or whatever else they need.

Bedtime Meditation: I Love You

Have you ever done a meditation or yoga class, come into your body, and then realized you're exhausted? For children who get amped up or tend to be dreamy, the "I Love You" Meditation helps them touch into their bodies, so they can relax and get to sleep.

It goes like this: As they lie in bed, have them say, "I love you, toes. I love you, feet. I love you, ankles…" all the way up through their entire body. If they are too young or too tired, you can say it for them. For children who keep chattering or fidgeting, just start on the "I love you…" until they realize it's bedtime. Even if they appear not to be participating, hearing your voice will cue them to relax each subsequent part of their body. Perhaps they'll go to sleep before you reach the head, and that's fine.

In addition to helping them unwind, this message of self-love is a wonderful way to end the day! Whatever enters the subconscious as we're going to sleep makes a big impact. As kids get to puberty and adulthood, this early experience of feeling good in their bodies should prove all the more meaningful.

Send Sparkles

Most of us naturally want to help and heal others. So, how do we do that without overextending or taking on problems that aren't ours? How do we do that in a way that honors other people? We'll delve into this in Chapter 9, "Energy Healing and Manifesting." For now, here is a simple exercise you can share with the kids in your life.

If someone is hurt or ill or upset, or when a loved one needs extra support to manifest a new home or job or other dream, we can send sparkles. For kids, I illustrate this by holding my hand in the air and wiggling my fingers. If the person who needs support is present, I'll point my fingers at them, but this works virtually just as well. "Let's send Grandma sparkles," I might say. And then, we can pick a colored light that this person needs, such as gold or pink. Almost any age child can do this with you.

This teaches children that when someone is in need, they are able to help. It resolves the imbalance between how much they feel and how much they can do, and this is soothing. Even better, they learn that they don't have to use their *own* energy to support another. The "sparkles" are in the air, so to speak. Depending on your belief system, you can teach them they come from God or angels or from the Universe. Watch your kids light up as they realize they can connect to Divine energy!

Guess Who?

This is a fun game I've played with my kids' Aikido classes. If you are a teacher or parent, you can do this whenever you have a group of children together. Make sure they know each other's names and have gotten to know each other, at least briefly.

Have one child stand facing a wall, with their back to the others and their arms by their sides. This person is "it." The rest stand quietly at least six feet back. Go ahead and tap one child on the head, which signals them to walk forward and hold the wrists of the person who's "it."

Now, without looking, "it" needs to guess who is grabbing them. Once they discover who it is or after a few turns each, someone new is chosen to be "it."

"Guess Who?" is a great way to explore how each person gives off a unique "vibe." It also teaches us about the importance of our "energy broadcast," as the "grabber" also learns that the way they show up influences the response they get. We innately know these things. The game makes them more real for kids as it also encourages them to pay attention.

Chapter 9:
ENERGY HEALING AND MANIFESTING

WHAT IS HEALING AND WHEN DO YOU DO IT?

True Healing Restores Wholeness

As you've been learning to read energy, perhaps you've wondered, "What do I do if I don't like what I see?" Good news—there is often something you can do. This final chapter will show you how to heal yourself or someone else.

So let's talk about what healing is and isn't. It is not about doing something for someone else. You don't have to get rid of anything or make anything happen. When you heal, you simply hold a vibration for someone to match. It's less about what you do and more about being in a space of wholeness. When you do this, healing occurs naturally.

Being in wholeness may sound lofty, but you don't have to be perfect. Anytime you are free from resistance in an area where another person has resistance, they will heal in your presence. You don't need to be more evolved than the person you're healing. It's not a competition with yourself or them. We all have blind spots and areas where we are challenged, as well as aspects of life that are easy for us.

Even when you and your healee have similar issues, you're inevitably more neutral about them than you are about yourself. For this reason, giving them a reading or healing can help you see straight where you've been stuck. To this point, you can also break your own patterns by doing energy work, or any activity that changes your perspective.

Unconscious Healing

When you begin to explore your capacity to heal, you'll probably discover many ways you've healed unconsciously. Any tendencies to take inappropriate responsibility for other people, or to heal with less than pure motivations will come up. Because we don't do this type of healing on purpose, it probably doesn't look like "healing." In fact, it may seem quite the opposite.

I knew a family where one of the four siblings was always sick. As an adult, she had a foul mouth and was difficult to be around. Her chronic health issues were such that others had to care for her child. She won the battle with cancer in her 20s, then died in her 30s when a heart transplant failed to take.

Looking at this psychically, she didn't just have bad luck. She was the family healer! What others didn't want to feel or didn't know how to work through, she absorbed like a sponge. Her body was filled with the vibration of the family's "garbage," and her inability to process it all resulted in illness and frustration. Because this energy was so ingrained, a healthy heart with a new vibration did not resonate in her body. This is an extreme example of what can happen when we take on others' pain unknowingly. Most of us have a much milder experience of being unconscious healers. Yet it's worth looking at.

If you're reading this, you are likely a natural healer, and I bet you started long before you had training! Be tender with yourself and keep practicing your psychic self-care as you learn new and improved ways to heal. By now, you have foundational tools for self-awareness, and each exercise to come will guide you to heal from a grounded place. Healing is about your vibration, the responsibility and choice you have to maintain it, and the gift you are offering as you hold it in the presence of others.

When Should You Heal?

1. Only with permission and only if the other person wants it. Ask first, don't assume. When they aren't available to ask (for instance, if they are ill or no longer in the body, or if someone in their life is requesting healing on their behalf), you can ask them psychically. We will get into this as we go.
2. Consciously, when you determine it's for the greatest good. By contrast, here are some ways we might be motivated by unhealed parts of ourselves. I suggest exploring and working through any of

the following common unconscious driving factors that you may discover in yourself:

- A need to be loved or needed
- The desire for power or validation
- A drive to control others so that you feel safe
- An attempt to avoid your own stuff through focus on the other person

Once you're clear in yourself, you can observe more about how to help another. Sometimes someone is receptive to healing, yet they have certain stubborn areas where they resist. Don't force healing in these cases. Instead, start where there is an opening, and then often you can circle back to the stubborn place. For example, their childhood wound may be excruciating in the moment, but they're eager to reclaim more self-worth. Focusing on what they can have today will eventually unearth and heal the buried trauma.

In other cases, someone feels powerless to even admit their current circumstances, but a relevant past life feels distant enough to look at. As I described her experience centuries ago in a different body, one client commented, "Are you sure you're not talking about this life?" I laughed and admitted that there may be parallels.

Another client came to me, and from my perspective, I didn't see anything too earth-shattering. Apparently, she liked the healing though, because next she sent her son. After that, she said, "Would you do a healing for my dog?"

I don't specialize in animals, but I said, "Sure." I felt that I could help somehow. And wow—that healing for her dog was more powerful than hers and her sons combined. It was as if the dog had taken on all of her disowned "stuff," and finally when I described how these powerful emotions were expressed through him, she got the healing she'd initially come for.

Sometimes your healee will hit a threshold where they have had enough. It's not always topic-related; they may just need time to process or integrate things. Practice sensing this and don't push. The times where we keep banging on a closed door may reveal our own issues. Have amusement and redirect yourself if this is the case. You are evolving.

Know that you may get triggered in a healing, just as in a reading. Be willing to pause and clear your energy. Be humble and willing to recognize your strengths and where you still have room to grow.

In this chapter, I'll guide you through various healing exercises for yourself. Feel free to use them for others as well; just be sure to begin and end each healing session using the methods noted in the previous section on reading others. For reference, this chapter merely scratches the surface on energy healing. If you enjoy learning to heal and would like to deepen your practice, see the resources at the end of the book for more information.

WRITING EXERCISE: WHEN HAVE YOU HEALED UNCONSCIOUSLY?

Write down all the times you can think of where you healed unconsciously. For example, you may include:

- Occasions where you simply held a vibration
- Times where you took responsibility for what was not yours
- Instances where your healing efforts were motivated by unhealed parts of yourself
- In each case, where were you coming from? Did it cause problems for yourself or others? Were there any benefits?

WRITING EXERCISE NOTES

MEDITATION: PREPARING TO HEAL

This is a meditation you can do before you heal another person, or just to clean up the way you heal in your everyday life. Is there someone you'd like to change or help? It would be great to consider how much they can receive! In addition, do this meditation before you offer an "official" healing using the exercises in this book.

Beyond other people, you can also use this practice to discover how much *you* can receive healing. If there's ever been something you wanted to change but couldn't, I'm about to give you a way to clear your own resistance. Find your cozy meditation spot, and let's begin:

- Sit with your feet flat on the floor, close your eyes, and relax your breathing.
- Ground yourself. Run your earth and cosmic energy.
- Create a magnetic, shiny soap bubble a few feet out in front of you.
- Allow this bubble to draw out of you anything that has caused you to heal unconsciously, or in unhelpful ways.
- Stay in your body and notice what goes into the bubble. Do you see pictures, get messages, or have sensations? Breathe and observe until this feels complete.
- Then, send your bubble out to the edge of the horizon. Watch from behind your eyes as it goes "poof" into a burst of light in the distance.
- Think of a time when you wanted to heal someone else.
- Imagine a gauge with a dial or display from 0-100%. Let it be at 0 or blank for now.
- Now ask, *How much can this person receive healing from me at this time?* See what percentage the gauge reflects, then let the gauge reset back to 0.
- Pick one specific area where you could use healing.
- Repeat the above exercise, asking the gauge to show you how much you're able to receive healing in this area now.
- Dissolve the gauge.

- Create one more soap bubble out in front of you, and then use it to clear any resistance you have to healing.
- Observe what you're clearing, then shoot the bubble into the distance and watch it burst into light.
- Recheck your grounding and energy flowing.
- Create a gold sun above your head, three times as big as your physical body. Let this sun attract all the light that you've given away or scattered beyond yourself. In addition, intend that it draws in all the healing energy you're ready to receive.
- Drink in the gold light as it flows through your body from head to toe, filling you in wherever you need it.

ADDRESSING HEALTH ISSUES

Some health problems are purely physical and many need to be addressed physically. However, most have emotional or spiritual components as well. Everything is connected, and this is the basis for holistic systems of care such as Ayurveda, chiropractic or Traditional Chinese Medicine. From these perspectives, we are not just looking to eradicate symptoms but instead to cultivate overall balance. I find these philosophies very resonant with my view of healing as restoring wholeness. When our bodies and energy bodies function properly, they can resolve most disruptions more easily.

What causes health issues? Why do we get sick? When my clients' bodies don't feel well, I frequently see the following:

- Unforgiveness of self or others
- Ancestral patterns
- Energy stagnation / lack of circulation
- Excessive, lacking or misapplied energy
- Negative mindset or vibration
- Past life karma

I could tell many stories for each of the above. For example, I saw that Sarah was clearing old grief out of her lungs, related to her mother. The next day, she reached out and told me she'd come down with a flu and cough. She felt her body was purging the energy I had seen. It was ancestral, and as she raised her vibration and committed to moving forward, the sadness and related symptoms got released.

Weak digestion is one form of lack of energy. This may occur when someone feels they can't process everything going on around them. Here, I'd work on supporting their presence in the third chakra and help them reclaim strength to manage their life. In supporting one's ability to "digest" their emotions, thoughts and input from the environment, physical digestion tends to improve in turn.

Heartburn or a churning gut can indicate misapplied mental energy.

This includes over-thinking instead of taking action, or perhaps trying to think our way through our feelings. Contrary to our popular culture, the mind shouldn't always lead the way. Our bodies revolt if the head tries to override the gut. To change this tendency, we can do energy work to redirect the mental energy back where it belongs, and simultaneously bring more awareness to the body and emotions. Techniques to calm the mind and nervous system also provide support.

Lack of circulation can reveal that you don't feel free to be all of you. Perhaps you fear what will happen if you are? One client gets migraines when life gets more joyful than she's accustomed to experiencing it. If someone has headaches or muscle knots, we'll look at why the energy is stuck. What are they holding onto or resisting? Are there stories, pictures or beliefs that limit this person's full expression? These can be released, transformed or replaced as applicable.

While there are many case-by-case nuances, here are some quick tips on how to heal health issues:

- Forgive and love
- Clear the karma (I'll share some techniques for this shortly!)
- Keep a positive vibration and focus
- Be present in your body so you can feel what it needs
- Use the "bubble" and other clearing practices to release emotions and energies affecting your health
- Choose a supportive environment and lifestyle (and perhaps, find a health care provider to supply personalized advice)

If you have specific health concerns, I recommend exploring how the relevant systems and functions in your body correspond to the energetic systems and functions. Much has been written about this, and it's fairly intuitive. Heart issues may relate to relationship challenges, a need for self-love, or a lacking sense of purpose and connection. Problems with elimination tend to indicate difficulties in letting go. Reproductive challenges tie in with creativity. I'm sure you can think of many more.

I am particularly fascinated with epigenetics, which is the study of how one's behavior and environment affect gene expression. While family history may play a role in our health, this science indicates that it need not limit us. The body's cells are constantly being renewed. So no matter the state of your health now, each choice you make along with your environment will make a difference. Small influences day by day add up to big changes over time.

From a spiritual perspective, some say we create our bodies out of our consciousness. I have seen this for instance with weight loss, where someone repeatedly visualized a certain number on the scale and then attained that weight. Does visualization alone cause weight loss? I don't think so. However, continually imprinting the mind with a certain picture may cause one to naturally make choices that support that goal. Especially if someone *feels as if* they've achieved their ideal weight, their self-love increases. Filled with satisfaction and a new sense of themselves, they'll be drawn to corresponding food and lifestyle choices—and this will likely change their bodies.

What about death? Our culture tends to see it as always bad, to be avoided at all costs. We tend not to want to look at aging or death, and yet these things are inevitable. I am sometimes asked about clients' elderly parents who are getting close to passing. While this can be emotional for the family, it's also a profound spiritual process to witness someone "wrapping things up." The transition of a loved one shows us that while the body is temporary, the soul's life is everlasting.

Many spiritual traditions say that how we die indicates how we are reborn. This is not just about the physical cause of death but also one's state of consciousness. Health issues may repeat in the next life, as well as spiritual or emotional tendencies. Knowing this, we can re-frame "health" to include health of one's whole being. We can stop running from death and instead focus on increasing peace and overall wellness.

WRITING EXERCISE: DISCOVERING THE ENERGY BEHIND YOUR HEALTH ISSUES

What are three health issues or things you'd like to improve about your body or physical energy? These can be small or large, acute or chronic:

1.

2.

3.

For each of the above, write about any emotions or energies you suspect may be affecting your body. Consider what that system or part of your body represents as well as what was going on in your life when it started. Perhaps close your eyes and ask that part of your body—or condition within your body—if it has a message for you. Note what you discover here:

1.

2.

3.

WHAT CAN YOU HEAL BESIDES PEOPLE?

For any place, event or situation, there is a field of energy. We saw this in learning to read a relationship using three roses. In addition, there are vibrational fields surrounding every business, project, building, group or event. You may wish to cleanse or energize your home or workplace, an important meeting, or some area of your life. For example, just as you did rose readings for your money, love life, career, etc., you can also heal various aspects of your life using the technique to follow.

Rather than simply hoping a situation will turn out ok, and in addition to using your intuition to assess a space or situation, you have the power to influence things to your favor. Of course, you cannot control others, but you can change what *you* experience. Warning: As you hold intention in this way, some people may leave your life, or your circumstances may change. This happens if your desired change is strong enough, and yet cannot be accommodated in your present reality.

PRACTICE: HEALING A SPECIFIC PROJECT, SPACE OR SITUATION

- Sit in meditation with your feet flat on the floor.
- Ground yourself and run your energy.
- Find the center of your head and claim your sanctuary space there.
- Smooth out and balance your aura.
- Consider something you would like to heal, besides yourself.
- Imagine a large, clear bubble a few feet out in front of you. Allow that bubble to represent your chosen project, event, situation, group or area of your life.
- As you picture the bubble, notice what's in it. What about this needs healing?
- Ground the bubble and clear anything out of the space that does not belong. Notice what's being cleared and let it go into the earth, or perhaps see it fly back to wherever it belongs.
- Next, energize the bubble by creating a magnetic golden sun above it. Allow this sun to reclaim all the energy that belongs in this space, and also attract anything that supports its greatest good.
- Once the sun is ready, pop it and let the liquid gold light flood the bubble.
- Send the bubble off as far as you can imagine.
- Think of this like a boomerang, bound to come back to you. Relax, knowing you have "placed your order" with the Universe.
- Fill yourself in with a gold sun, and then come out of meditation.

READING AND HEALING THE PAST OR FUTURE

As you read the energy around a situation, you may wonder about the past or future. For example, someone's current issues often relate to childhood experiences, so it's useful to be able to look back along a timeline for what age the early triggers occurred. On the other hand, looking forward allows us to see the likely outcome of various choices, as well as probable dates when circumstances will shift.

Going back before childhood, ancestral patterns are commonly at the root of deep-seated issues. To examine these, you can use a timeline for Mom's side of the family as well as a timeline for Dad's side.

Do we have multiple timelines? Yes, I think life is a choose-your-own-adventure journey. If you don't like what you see on your current timeline, perhaps you need to make some different choices today. The next meditation will go over how to use a timeline to read and heal.

PRACTICE: READING AND HEALING TIMELINES

- Consider a current challenge or desire you have.
- Sit in meditation, ground yourself, and observe your inhalations and exhalations.
- Run your earth and cosmic energy.
- Look out from the center of your head and imagine a timeline for this challenge or desire. See today in the middle of the timeline.
- Ask if there are past experiences affecting your current challenge. Let them show up as spots on the timeline. Perhaps you see a year, an age, or a picture or symbol about what occurred. Take in the impressions you receive.
- What else do you see in the past? These could be one-time memories or periods of years with a certain "flavor" to them. Get curious about how they've affected you.
- When you feel ready, send golden light backwards from today. This heals the past so you can have more of what you desire now.
- Do you have questions about the future? Take a look forward on the timeline to see if any notable images show up. Are there certain months or years that "light up"? What do you sense happening at these times?
- If you don't like the future you see, ask for insight as to how to change it. Are there shifts in your thinking, behavior or energy that will steer the future towards a different course? Breathe and pay attention to what you receive on this.
- As with the past, you can send gold light forward to clear obstacles and energize the future. Go ahead and do this now. If you like, add in any colors or intentions that feel supportive.
- When you're ready, dissolve your timeline and fill yourself in with a golden sun.

WHY DO PAINFUL SCENARIOS REPEAT?

As trauma happens, whether one time or ongoing, we go into survival. From an energy perspective, we check out in order to cope. While this always leaves us vulnerable, checking out is particularly dangerous when we're in survival. This is because we not only absorb whatever energy is in the environment, we *confuse it with survival information.* The very source of the abuse, shock or pain seems like *what we need* in order to survive. Of course, this is backwards, but this is one reason—from my psychic view—that people keep choosing the same toxic scenarios over and over. They know better but cannot seem to help themselves. It's not conscious.

In order to get free of these patterns, we need to clear the past pain but also replace it with healthy energy that truly supports us. This is why we always bring in gold suns after releasing energy. There are other ways you can reprogram yourself, such as affirmations, embodiment practices (such as yoga, dance, chi gong or other forms of movement), and therapeutic treatments and remedies. I recommend exploring these if you feel the need.

PRACTICE: HOW TO CLEAR KARMA WITH A CERTAIN PERSON OR ISSUE

You have learned to read a past life, but how do you heal the karma? The following technique gives you a way to do just that. You can use it for a specific lifetime you know about; however, it's not necessary to see your past lives to make use of this exercise. If there is a person with whom you have an intense connection, or a repeating pattern in your life that you can't seem to fix, karma may have something to do with it. So let's do some clearing!

- Sit with your feet on the floor and ground your body.
- Find your sanctuary space behind your eyes.
- Run your earth and cosmic energy. Watch as showers of light flow out the top of your head and hands.
- Now, consider something with which or someone with whom you would like to heal your karma. You may wish to end a repeating pattern or find more freedom in relationship to that person.
- As you breathe, ask if you have unresolved past lives with regards to this person, place, group or situation.
- A few feet out in front of you, imagine a ring that represents the answer to your question. If you have "unfinished business" in the area of your inquiry, the ring will have a gap in it. It will not be a full circle. See if there is a gap, and if so, how large it is. The size of the gap will indicate how much unresolved karma you have.
- If you see a full circle, perhaps ask about something or someone else.
- Once you discover some karma to clear, spin the ring in your mind's eye until you shut the gap. See the ring as complete.
- Once you see a full circle with no gaps, toss this ring out to the Universe and let it dissolve.
- Fill in with a gold sun, in particular calling your energy back from that lifetime, karmic situation or person.

THE POWER OF FORGIVENESS

Often difficult to do, forgiveness is one of the most powerful ways to heal yourself. Even when you know it's the right thing to do, even when you know it's for your own good, it can feel nearly impossible when you're just not ok with something that's happened.

If we entertain the thought that all dis-ease comes down to lack of circulation, it's apparent that not being able to let go of something creates stagnation. So how do we do this necessary thing?

For me, it's helped to "give things to God" when I don't understand them and can't make peace. If you prefer, you can substitute the word "God" with "the Divine" or "the Universe." When my human self feels pain, I still know that the Universe has a plan—something perhaps I have yet to see. I have had enough life experience to recognize this.

Feeling empowered allows us to forgive. Otherwise, if we feel helpless in the midst of pain, it's more appealing to go numb. Finding hope that life will get better, such as filling your life with new and positive experiences, can make forgiving feel ok. In addition, you may need lots of self-care and positive self-talk to boost your spirits.

At some point, looking at your part in a painful situation will also bring empowerment and freedom. Don't force it if you feel too raw. Once you have the capacity, consider if there was something you got out of a difficult situation. Earlier, I shared a meditation to clear your subconscious reasons for taking on others' energy.

I also recommend journaling to explore this. For example, some years ago I wrote a letter to my college boyfriend, forgiving him and taking responsibility for my part in what had happened between us. I never sent the letter and, in fact, I wrote it at a car wash. As they waved at me to let me know my car was ready, a man came up and asked me out! Single at the time, I had written the letter to free myself from any baggage in my love life so I could attract someone new. I didn't end up dating the car wash guy, but I took note of the instant manifestation. To this day, I have no doubt in the impact of forgiveness. In particular, by taking responsibility for my part, I set myself free when I saw how I chose the situation. Of course, abuse is not ok, and we don't consciously invite tragedies. However, to whatever degree you can see your lessons and benefits within difficult circumstances, you see how powerful you are. You see how generous, creative and abundant life really is. And then, why not forgive?

WRITING EXERCISE: OWNING YOUR PART AND SETTING YOURSELF FREE

Think about a situation in your life where you have not fully forgiven. Perhaps that's a person who "did you wrong." Maybe it's yourself—if you know you could have handled something better. Once you have chosen a person or situation, write about what happened with the motivation to discover your part in the matter. What drew you to participate? What were you getting out of doing so? Own this part. Even if you still condemn what happened, finding your agency here will bring healing. Go ahead and write.

WRITING EXERCISE NOTES

HOW TO HANDLE INTERFERENCE

Sometimes you'll find obstacles to healing yourself or someone else. Beyond patiently working with someone's human levels of readiness, interference requires more awareness and skill. Knowing what causes these obstacles and how to identify and work with them comes in handy. Otherwise, they can be very frustrating!

Interference says, "No, don't heal!" It may go as far to say, "If you heal, I'll die." It's like a parasite in your body that freaks out if you decide to cleanse. Generally, these energies come from entities and not from a person's true self. They will create all kinds of distractions to prevent you from discovering them or booting them out.

As you practice healing, the interference may show up around you, around the person you're attempting to heal, or from the environment. Remember that no matter how things seem, the interference is not you, and it's not who the other person really is. It wants you to believe in smoke and mirrors, but you'll only get anywhere if you look deeper. Ask in meditation and see if you can locate the source.

Know that whoever experiences interference has somehow agreed to it. You can look at why, as well as their level of openness in how you communicate about it. Generally, being delicate and keeping a sense of humor will allow you to address things more easily.

Here are some different ways interference might show up:

- Seeing black or "nothing"
- Feeling stuck or blocked
- Hearing, seeing or sensing "Don't look"
- Missing appointments, constantly changing appointments, arriving late or having crises right when it's time to heal
- Dropped calls, lost connections, static or other technical issues
- Too much talking without listening or allowing space for healing

If someone is stuck in a mental place, they may be talking and processing but not hearing you. They could be asking rapid-fire questions in an attempt to soothe their anxiety, but not really dropping beneath the surface enough to actually feel better. In these cases, you can suggest re-framing their story or questions. Even better, ask them if they'd like a healing. Let them know it will clear the way so they can have what they're really wanting.

Whether or not your client wants a healing, if there is a being or person standing in the way of your connection, you can always ground the "interferer" and send them to the light. This does not break your client's agreement with that being, but simply creates space so you two can relate without interference. Then if your client is open to it, you can tell them what you saw, and look at why they agreed to let that energy in.

Intention setting can preemptively reduce interference. If you're getting a lot of interference, you may need to strengthen your intention and grounding as a general practice. As you advance with your healing, you may not need to do this for every session because you are continuously in your intention. This goes for other energy tools as well. However, if you start to have trouble, always come back to the basics.

On occasion, interference can be divine protection. We humans don't always want what's best for us! Sometimes, there are just things we can't see and so it's good to be humble. If you suspect some roadblock is really serving you, ask intuitively if this is the case. If so, do your best to be amused, curious and appreciative!

UNDERSTANDING UNHELPFUL MEDIUMSHIP AND HOW TO WORK WITH IT

With interference, unhelpful mediumship is the likely culprit. This is, basically, channeling something you didn't mean to channel—in particular, a negative or energy-draining spirit. Most all of us do this to some degree, and it's easy to do, especially if these beings relate to family patterns or deep-seated wounds. They can hang around us for decades unseen, and we can live with them just fine to a point, like having parasites in the body. However, it's optimal to find them and clear them out. Remembering that mediumship is the ability to enter and leave a medium (your body), you get to decide how you are owning that space as well as how you share it.

Channeling sounds glamorous. However, so much of it is actually unhealthy. Your spirit is meant for your body. You chose the perfect body based on your soul's desires for evolution. Having your body allows you to enjoy life, express your purpose and learn lessons—all in ways that you cannot do without a body.

The beings that wish to channel through you have one thing that you do not. They have freedom from the body and the density that goes with it. This gives them a perspective that may be useful to you. You can touch into that space while consciously meditating out of your body (such as in the "Running White" meditation we covered earlier), dreaming or daydreaming— yet they reside there. It's very important to remember that this does not make them enlightened. Just because they have perspective doesn't mean they have healed themselves enough to be of service coming into your field.

While spirits may have a fresh outlook to offer you, you have something very important that they do not. This is your body! We spend so much time being annoyed with our bodies—including our aches and pains, our mental and emotional patterns, and the grind of work and tasks—that we forget how incredible they are. Without them, we could not enjoy food, sex, touch, movement and all of our physical experiences. They enable us to actualize our purpose and to create, speak and clear our karma. This is why we reincarnate, because we need the vehicle of a body to work through things.

So, when a spirit comes to channel through you, it's likely because *you* have something they need or want, not the other way around. This is not always "bad," for example a musical spirit that uses your hands to play piano. Even if they aren't more evolved than you, they still bring beauty. In other cases, they want your body for sex, alcohol or expressions of rage. You'll notice at times it feels like something "comes through you." When this happens, ask yourself how you like it, and whether you want to keep doing it.

We all want to check out at times. We disengage from our bodies to avoid pain, to feel safe, or to experience a sense of expansion. The problem when we leave at a "low" vibration is that we bring in energy that matches this vibration. If you leave because you're sad, you are a magnet for more sadness. Channeling because you don't feel capable on your own will bring in beings that need validation. In each instance, the energy you attract reinforces the pain pattern instead of healing it. In short, it backfires.

As you work towards reclaiming your space and clearing out the beings and energies that came in when you left, you may "space out" or feel dreamy or sleepy. This is because you were unconscious in the past, in moments of pain or unawareness when these patterns began. To heal them, you have to move these pockets of unconsciousness out of your field, which means you'll likely feel unconscious in the process. This is actually a good sign. It does not mean that you're slacking off!

Who do we channel and why? Sometimes we bring in our ancestors, who recognize and attach to us to perpetuate certain patterns. They feel so familiar it can be hard to recognize or get rid of them, yet it can be done. Other spirits you pick up may seem "random." Perhaps you went to a bar, coffee shop or festival and your space felt trashed afterwards. You likely picked someone up! Think of them like flies. As someone who is spiritually open, your head looks like a light bulb everywhere you go. You attract them. Besides departed souls, it's also possible to bring in trans-medium energy from someone who's alive, or to bring in a vibrational pattern from the collective. Know that you are highly desirable and capable in the arena of mediumship, even if you are just learning about it.

I'm sure you have people in your life who channel as well. Most of us have way more beings around than we realize, and they drive us in unconscious ways. The subtle ways they impact personality are rarely obvious, while the more dramatic experiences can cause havoc in the lives of everyone around them! So it's good to know how to identify and work with these energies when you encounter them. Here are a few signs to look for:

- A person isn't acting like themselves. They may have an addiction or tend to be "moody."
- Someone is magnetic and attracts a lot of attention (even when they're quiet).
- Destructive, chaotic or sabotaging energies
- Highly inspired creativity or speech that feels "larger than life"

How do you stay grounded around others who are channeling negative energies? Here are some tips:

- Talk to the person who owns the body, not to the being they are channeling. Sometimes that "brings them back," especially if you use their name. At the very least, you won't get so pulled into the being's vortex this way.
- Use your meditation tools before going around these people or into public spaces.
- Raise your vibration! You will only attract what you are a match for. This is why being a bright light is not necessarily a problem. However, as an intuitive person, you have a responsibility to keep a positive focus if you'd like to keep out the riffraff.

If you have a tendency towards unconscious mediumship, how do you manage it? Some possibilities are:

- Watch your diet. Protein can be important for grounding. Minimize or eliminate alcohol, caffeine and sugar, and be mindful of how you use them. The same goes for any addictions, distractions or preoccupations.
- More grounding. Get out on the earth.
- Feel your feelings. A desire to avoid pain will push you out of the body, which makes you more vulnerable to negativity.
- Be more aware of the vibrations you surround yourself with. This includes foods, music, TV, movies, neighborhoods, friends, etc.

If a being gets in your space and you do something you aren't proud of, who is responsible? You are! Oops. It was your body that did it, and so it's your body that needs to make amends and correct the situation. You are left with the karma. This is all the more reason we need to be discerning when it comes to channeling.

This next meditation will guide you to clear up any tendencies you have towards unhelpful mediumship.

MEDITATION: HEALING YOUR UNHELPFUL MEDIUMSHIP AGREEMENTS

- Sit with your feet on the floor and ground yourself.
- Consciously soften on your exhales and sit taller on your inhales.
- Run your earth and cosmic energy, and please notice the showers of colored light cleansing your aura bubble.
- Now, from the center of your head, look up at your crown chakra and allow it to turn all white.
- Pop up to the 12 o'clock position at the back of your crown. Imagine taking a seat there.
- From this point, see your white loop flowing down the back and up the front, in a continuous circuit. Include your first creative ring, just above the crown chakra.
- Go a few feet up and behind your body. Watch your white loop from there as you cross your legs and release your grounding cord.
- Next, look for one being or vibrational pattern in your space that is not helpful. Look first for the being or energy's color, then allow yourself to see more and receive more information about it. Ask questions like: "How does this affect me?" "What are the signs when it's in my space?" and "How long has this been around?"
- Ask yourself if you are ready to let this being or energy go.
- If so, ground it and see it flying up to the light, out of your field.
- Next ask, "Why did I agree to let this energy in? What was I getting out of it?" Notice the answers you receive.
- Was this a one-time thing, or have you had an agreement to bring this energy in? If you still sense an agreement, would you like to release it?
- If so, imagine the contract you've had with this being or energy. Can you see what it says? Now, update it. Rewrite it so it works for you today, stamp it "VOID," burn it or use some other creative way to complete it. Then, send the agreement to the light.
- Using your white energy, clear any remaining energy in your field that agreed to channel what you just released.

- Reclaim your trans-medium channels on the left and right sides of your spine. Reset them to your own white vibration.
- When you're done, come back to the 12:00 position on your crown chakra.
- Bring your crown to gold, place your feet back on the floor and re-ground your body.
- Come into the center of your head and run your earth and cosmic energy.
- Fill in with a gold sun. Notice how you feel as you open your eyes.

CYCLES OF CREATION

As discussed earlier in the section on creative rings, there are three cycles within the creative process. To make sense of how they each play out in daily life, here is an overview of their primary functions:

1. **Create**—The spark within you that initiates. This can include new projects and goals, business ventures, pregnancy, new hobbies, artistic pursuits, gardening, cooking.
2. **Destroy**—Releasing what no longer serves. This can mean cleansing your body or home, transforming unhelpful beliefs or toxic emotions, letting go of a relationship or a job or a lifestyle, choosing to forgive.
3. **Maintain**—Taking care of what you have and translating consciousness into form. Think of your lifestyle habits, time spent with your loved ones, spiritual practice, exercise, managing your money, maintaining your home or vehicle, receiving health checkups and treatments, and carrying out your plans.

Starting new things tends to be exciting and popular, and so our culture prizes creation. Some of us feel enslaved by duties and routines, and so procrastinate around maintaining our lives. Carrying out tasks can be boring, though certain personalities love the comforts of routine. Many of us avoid destroying anything, yet for some—often trans-medium types—this is addictive or compulsive. We reward bigger-better-faster, and we resist letting go. For example, we learn not to talk about death, divorce or other losses, and so may not give these processes the attention they need.

We are generally in just one of these cycles in any given moment. It's important to know which one you're in, because it's difficult to create when you're in "letting go" mode or vice versa. For the most part, you'll find more ease and success when you honor whatever cycle you're in until it shifts. Not every day or season is going to be exciting or comfortable.

Being conscious of where your energy is will also ensure you don't misapply it. If you're unaware of being in a "creative" cycle, you may create things you weren't planning on. It's the same with "destroying." Conscious letting go is an amazing boost to your creative power, whereas destroying when you didn't mean to can cause harm. It's also important not to gloss over the "maintaining" cycle. It's needed in order to keep what we have, and to build strength so we can let go and eventually create again.

To create anything, we need to utilize all three aspects. If we start projects constantly and never let go of anything, we have no space to receive what we truly desire. If we don't maintain our lives and possessions, they fall apart. By contrast, when we tend to what we have, we signal the Universe that we're ready for more. And if we are hooked on drama, always destroying something or always in a healing process, we don't get anywhere either!

Next, I'll share a writing exercise to help you see how to apply this in your life.

WRITING EXERCISE: DISCOVERING HOW YOU CREATE YOUR LIFE

Which cycle are you in now—create, destroy or maintain? Circle it, below. Then, write about your relationship to each aspect:

1. **Create**
2. **Destroy**
3. **Maintain**

KEYS TO MANIFESTING

You've come so far in harnessing the power of your energy. You've learned tools to see, hear and know psychically. Your ability to receive is inseparable from your ability to project. And your life is a dance within the cycles of create-destroy-maintain.

Seeking psychic advice, healing or training is not an end in and of itself. We want this support so we can realize better lives. So let's talk now about how we use energy to manifest. In my experience, here are some of the keys:

- Self-Worth
- Healthy Boundaries
- Appreciation
- Celebration
- Pleasure
- Presence

Self-Worth

To create a great life, we have to feel like we deserve it. Otherwise, we'll create and destroy. This may seem exciting at times, but we won't be able to keep a good thing going.

Our state of self-worth is not always obvious. With low self-esteem, we may subconsciously do things to push our good away. Six common ways to do this are: (1) being scattered or ungrounded, (2) rushing or showing up unprepared, (3) diminishing our greatness, (4) being in fantasy, (5) over-striving and (6) lack of self-care.

Low self-worth can look like hanging onto old patterns, even when they don't serve us. Here, we tend to hoard objects, relationships or beliefs that undermine our greatness.

When you're ready to up-level your life, anything you've been doing based on a lesser picture of yourself becomes glaringly obvious. This might include letting someone treat you poorly, spending your time on things you don't enjoy, working for too little pay, over-giving, keeping things that are worn out or that you don't love, or not cleaning or maintaining your home, car, body or relationships. What do you agree to (directly or indirectly) that is out of alignment with your worth?

Healthy Boundaries

Healthy boundaries tell the Universe what to send you. If you're open to whatever, you get whatever. You are not less spiritual when you have boundaries. A "yes" to everything ends up being a "no" to your deepest desires. As humans bound by time and space, we must discern. This life is precious.

Discernment is not judgement; discernment is a Divine quality. Of course, be flexible enough to receive something better than you've thought of. Be fluid as to how things arrive. Have enough amusement so you don't get tripped up by life's surprises and people's idiosyncrasies.

Clarity is like a laser beam to your dreams that creates ease. You are aligned with that thing and so you attract it. What you don't agree to won't find you; it will be demagnetized away. Healthy boundaries make your life easier.

Appreciation

What good is manifesting if you don't appreciate? Without giving thanks, you'll feel empty and keep grasping. This is an addictive state that the advertising industry would prefer you keep. I recommend shifting your focus to having and giving.

There is that saying, "When the student is ready, the teacher appears." So, how do you get ready? My teacher's answer was "Practice what you already know." This is another way of saying, "Have what you have." The more you do, the more you will receive.

If you give someone a compliment or a gift and they dismiss or ignore it, do you want to give another one? The Universe is just like you. Life is always giving, as long as we appreciate and make use of what is ours.

Financial gurus say we attract more abundance when we have savings. Perhaps because it helps us relax, money in the bank is like a magnet! In life, the same principle applies. Even if you don't have a lot, start appreciating it and be ready for the floodgates to open!

Celebration

After a big success or blessing, do you celebrate? Celebration is a higher octave of appreciation, a very attractive vibration.

I tend to receive money and opportunities when I take time off to play. I guess because I am in the business of helping people feel better, people are drawn to me when I feel good. They may not consciously know what I'm doing. However, since everyone is psychic, I imagine they think of me and say to themselves, "I want what she's having."

On every level, celebration brings blessings. By contrast, not stopping to appreciate your successes turns life into a grind. If you're never satisfied, always pushing towards the next goal, I bet you're just as hard on the people around you as you are on yourself. In this state, not only are you closed off to receiving, but people don't really want to be around you. And most of our opportunities come from people.

Celebration also says, "I'm worth it!"

Pleasure

Pleasure is a gateway to presence. Just as pain pushes us to disassociate, pleasure beckons us to be here now. And *here* is where we manifest.

This is why people paradoxically lose weight when they stop being so strict with their diets. Enjoying yourself means you stay in your body, which leads to healthier choices because you notice how your choices make you feel. And as soon as you start feeling good, junk food just doesn't make sense anymore. On a similar note, hang out with people who treat you well and see how much you still want to put up with your abusive boss or boyfriend. Good feelings build on themselves.

Emotions are also the fuel behind our manifesting. We can visualize and speak affirmations until the cows come home. But if we don't believe ourselves, it won't work. Have you ever made plans with a friend that you didn't really want to do, and then the plans fell through? This is because emotions trump words and ideas. It's amazing to witness life's feedback this way! This is why we need to feel our feelings, so we don't get stuck. And when it comes to pleasure, speaking or thinking about something you desire *while also feeling good* about it will activate your powers of attraction.

Presence

When the call you've been waiting for comes in, you still need to answer. Float off in your dreams all you want, but to bring them into physical reality, you need to be there ready. It may seem tedious. However, tending to the day-to-day creates a landing pad for your desires to anchor into your life. I'm thinking of something my yoga teacher told me when I first got my teaching certificate. He advised, "If nobody shows up for your class, don't leave. Stay and practice." By the time he gave me this advice, he was regularly drawing 70 people per class. He suggested that his early dedication to this physical practice was foundational to his success. It told the Universe he was serious.

People want to feel that you're for real. Whether they're considering hiring you for a job, dating you, or renting you an apartment, your presence makes you trustable. And so, you are chosen.

CONCLUSION

You have been psychic all your life. Hopefully, this book has opened you to a world you didn't know you knew so well. Most schools don't teach us about energy, and much of life does not validate it as real. If you've read this far, I trust you know very well how real it is.

Now what? I recommend daily practice, even if it's just the grounding and gold sun exercises. Some people ask me how I find the discipline to meditate every day. To me, that's like asking why I take regular showers. I don't feel as good if I don't! And for those who wonder how to find the time, I truly believe that working with energy saves us time because we stop processing so much of what's not ours. We can use our intuition to see which paths will be most joyful, efficient and successful. Why suffer when you have superpowers?

Of course, being psychic does not protect you from being human. It will not instantly erase your karma or make everyone around you behave the way you wish. If only! This is where being spiritual is also important. This is where the values of amusement, neutrality, compassion and ethics come in. The psychic path can be a path to evolution, but you must choose it to be.

I wouldn't want it any other way. This has been such a deep and rich path, and I'm honored to have so many profound conversations with fascinating souls. I don't take it lightly that people trust me with their personal challenges, experiences and dreams. I have seen so many transformations in my clients that I cannot doubt the meaning of this work.

There is so much light emerging in humanity at this time, and so much more openness to the world of intuition than there was when I started learning. I envision aspects of this material being woven into school curriculums and family dinners. I trust that we are ready to use this power wisely, and that those who are meant to do so will find their way.

RESOURCES

Find me on social media @annobrienliving.

Visit www.AnnOBrienLiving.com to learn more about classes, Intuitive Training Programs, and private sessions and to join my mailing list. Scan this QR code to go to my website now:

YOUR INTUITION JOURNAL

Intuition Journal

Intuition Journal

Intuition Journal

Intuition Journal

Intuition Journal

Intuition Journal

Intuition Journal

Intuition Journal

Intuition Journal

Intuition Journal

Intuition Journal

Intuition Journal

Intuition Journal

Intuition Journal

Intuition Journal

Intuition Journal

Intuition Journal

Intuition Journal

Intuition Journal

Intuition Journal

Intuition Journal

Intuition Journal

www.ingramcontent.com/pod-product-compliance
Lightning Source LLC
Chambersburg PA
CBHW060353080526
44583CB00012B/295